AA

M I N I G U I D E

New York

GW00722710

CONISTONE MOOR

Author: John Morrison
Verifier: David Winpenny
Managing Editor: Paul Mitchell
Art Editor: Carole Philp
Editor: Sandy Draper
Cartography provided by the Mapping Services Department of AA Publishing
Internal colour reproduction: Michael Moody

Produced by AA Publishing
© Automobile Association Developments Limited 2007

Published by AA Publishing (a trading name of Automobile Association Developments Limited,
whose registered office is Fanum House, Basing View, Basingstoke, Hampshire RG21 4EA; registered
number 1878835).

A03033F

TRADE ISBN-13: 978-0-7495-5592-4
SPECIAL ISBN-13: 978-0-7495-5699-0

A CIP catalogue record for this book is available from the British Library.

The contents of this book are believed correct at the time of printing. Nevertheless, the publishers
cannot be held responsible for any errors or omissions or for changes in the details given in this
book or for the consequences of any reliance on the information it provides. We have tried to ensure
accuracy in this book, but things do change and we would be grateful if readers would advise us of
any inaccuracies they may encounter. This does not affect your statutory rights.

Visit AA Publishing's website www.theAA.com/travel

Colour reproduction by Keene Group, Andover.
Printed in China by Everbest.

CONTENTS

The word 'moors' conjures up the image of a bleak, lonely and windswept landscape? Not the North York Moors. From the sharp escarpments in the west to the towering cliffs and sandy beaches on the east coast, the Moors offers a rich variety of landscapes, and attractions to please everyone. The heart of the North York Moors – designated a National Park more fifty years ago to protect this fragile and important area – is the plateau of hills that glow with a soft-purple wash of heather in the late summer. This is England's largest expanse of heather, and one of the must-see sights. You can walk for miles along old drovers' tracks that will take you past mysterious ancient earthworks and mounds and the medieval moorland crosses that are a familiar feature of the 'tops'. In all seasons, and most weathers, the North York Moors holds its fascination.

Thrusting into this high land are deep and densely wooded valleys, including Bransdale, with some of the area's remote farming communities; Farndale, famous for wild daffodils; and Rosedale, with remnants of the iron-working industry in a divine setting. Many of the area's most attractive towns and villages, such as Hutton-le-Hole and Lastingham, lie in the valleys.

Southwest of the central moorland are the gentler Howardian Hills, where picturesque abbeys – Rievaulx and Byland – and ruined castles like Helmsley rise from wooded valleys. North again around the Cleveland Hills, villages like Swainby and Great Ayton – where Captain Cook was schooled – huddle beneath the humpbacks of the hills.

Deep forests occupy much of the southeastern quarter of the area, with walks, mountain-bike trails and picnic sites set out among the trees. And strung along the glorious coast, from Staithes to Scarborough, are some of Britain's highest cliffs,

coves where smugglers landed contraband, idyllic fishing villages that appear to tumble headlong into the waves, and bracing headlands. Whitby, with its abbey, quirky church, Dracula connections and memories of its whaling past, is fascinating, while Scarborough lives up to its name as 'Queen of the Coast' with everything for a traditional, seaside holiday, from beaches to a huge castle just asking to be explored.

Walking is certainly one of the best ways to see the North York Moors. Large areas are unvisited by roads, and some of the best landscape is only accessible on foot. The roads tend to follow the tops of the ridges, leaving the valleys and deep forest to be discovered. But the Moors has something to offer everyone. And if you're looking for peace and quiet, that is as plentiful here as fresh air, too – just as it was during the 12th century when St Aelred, Abbot of Rievaulx, wrote that it offers 'a marvellous freedom from the tumult of the world'.

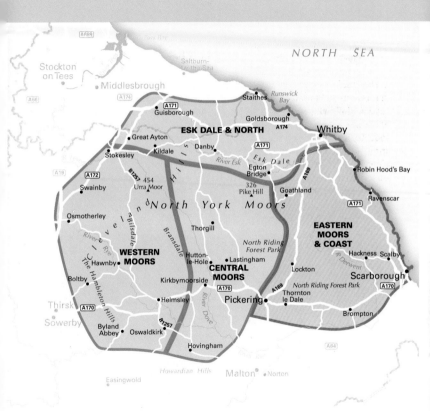

11

ESSENTIAL SPOTS

Enjoy superb views across the Vale of York from the top of Sutton Bank... walk part (or all!) of the Cleveland Way, which starts at Helmsley and ends at Filey Brigg on the coast...visit Staithes, a perfect example of an old Yorkshire fishing village...search Whitby's many antique shops for jet or watch it being made in the craftsmens' workshops or go in hunt of Bram Stoker's *Dracula*...look for a small carved mouse, Robert Thompson's unique trademark, on the furniture in local churches and visit the workshops at Kilburn...admire the thousands of daffodils at Farndale in springtime and linger by the extensive remains of Rievaulx Abbey...steam along the rails on the North Yorkshire Moors Railway, which runs from Pickering to Grosmont...look out for the lovely stone crosses that litter the moors...walk along the Roman road in Wheeldale in the footsteps of Roman soldiers...take the scenic Newtondale Forest Drive through North Riding Forest.

1

1 Rievaulx Abbey
The supeb ruins of Rievaulx Abbey, set in a magnificent wooded valley of the River Rye.

2 Hutton-le-Hole
Neat, flower-bedecked houses of mellow local stone, grouped around a tidy green that extends the length of the village, make Hutton-le-Hole a candidate for the title of Yorkshire's prettiest village.

13

3 Staithes

The village of Staithes is a delight to explore. Its position, wedged between steep-sided cliffs and Cowbar Beck, resulted in an attractive jumble of house building.

4 Robin Hood's Bay

The pretty little fishing village of Robin Hood's Bay is a tumble of brightly painted cottages that seem to stagger their way along the narrow roads towards the sea.

5 Farndale

The remote valley of Farndale, with its maze of narrow winding lanes and patchwork of fields, is where you can experience moorland scenery at its most beautiful.

6 Stone Crosses
Young Ralphs Cross, standing tall at a junction of roads near Rosedale Head, is the symbol of the North York Moors National Park. It is just one of many ancient stones and crosses found on these moors.

7 Egton Bridge
A tranquil corner at Egton Bridge. This pretty little village is set the lush woodland of the Esk Valley.

7

Day One in North York Moors

For many people a weekend break or a long weekend is a popular way of spending their leisure time. These pages offer a loosely planned itinerary designed to ensure that you make the most of your time, whatever the weather, and see and enjoy the very best of the area.

Friday Night

Stay at the Feversham Arms, Helmsley. This is a charming hotel located just a few yards from the Market Square with its own swimming pool and luxurious four-poster beds in many of the rooms. The restaurant is renowned for its good food (especially shellfish and game in season) and outstanding wine list.

Saturday Morning

Your first stop should be the Tourist Information Centre in the castle, for details of events happening during the weekend. A short drive north from Helmsley, on the B1257, you'll find the remains of Rievaulx Abbey to explore, one of Yorkshire's architectural gems, in a valley of the River Rye. Minor roads (make sure you have an atlas to hand) lead southwest to the fine Yorkshire village of Kilburn. Beneath the distinctive hill figure of the White Horse is the showroom of Robert Thompson's Craftsmen, whose work keeps alive the tradition and artistry of the famous 'Mouseman'. Opposite to the showroom is the visitor centre.

Saturday Lunch

Drive the short distance eastwards to the picturesque Byland Abbey where, directly opposite the ruins, you'll find the Abbey Inn. The stone-flagged floor, antique furniture and imaginative menu make this the ideal place for lunch.

Saturday Afternoon

Pass Helmsley once again and continue east along the A170 to Pickering, the terminus of the North Yorkshire Moors Railway. This preserved line offers a nostalgic return to the age of steam. A round trip to Goathland will show you some of the finest scenery in the North York Moors National Park, as well as giving you time to explore the moorland village perhaps now best known as a location for the TV series *Heartbeat*. On your return to Pickering, drive north up the A169, passing the huge natural amphitheatre known as the Hole of Horcum, towards the port of Whitby.

Day Two in North York Moors

Our second and final day starts with a visit to the bustling resort of Whitby and a nearby picturesque fishing village, before driving along the beautiful Esk Valley and across the moors, passing through a number of lovely villages, before arriving back in Helmsley.

Sunday Morning

Explore Whitby on foot. It's a fascinating town, with surprises at every turn in its winding streets. The abbey, St Mary's Church, the Captain Cook Museum and the harbour are just a few of the 'musts'. On a different scale are the tiny fishing villages of Staithes (north of Whitby) and Robin Hood's Bay (a few miles to the south). Both are achingly picturesque; take time to explore one or the other. Afterwards, a leisurely drive along the beautiful Esk Valley,

passing the lovely of villages of Grosmont, Glaisdale (look out for the Beggar's Bridge) and Lealholm will bring you to Danby. At the Moors Centre you can learn how the moorland landscape came to look the way it does, and perhaps have a cup of coffee. Drive south from Danby, along Blakey Ridge (this is on an unclassified road, more map reading needed). With the valley of Rosedale to your left and Farndale to your right, this is moorland scenery at its very best.

CASTLETON RIGG

Sunday Lunch

Look out for the Lion Inn, miles from anywhere on Blakey Ridge, where travellers have long received a warm welcome. Our suggested itinerary should make this a late lunch. No problem, the Lion Inn serves its excellent meals throughout the day.

Sunday Afternoon

Continue driving along Blakey Ridge, with perhaps a moorland walk to fill the lungs with pure upland air. Look out for the guide stones on the roadside. The road brings you to Hutton-le-Hole, one of Yorkshire's picture-postcard villages and well worth exploring. Near by is the equally pretty Lastingham.

Our weekend started with one monastic gem and ends with another intriguing religious site. The church at Lastingham has a 'secret' crypt, built almost a thousand years ago. Drive west along the A170 to arrive back in Helmsley where you can enjoy some afternoon tea before heading for home.

SLEDALE

Esk Dale & North

INTRODUCTION

The River Esk meanders from its source at moorland Westerdale via a number of villages before dividing the port of Whitby into two. The National Park's Visitor Centre, at Danby is the perfect spot for a riverside stroll and to learn about the unique moorland habitats of the Park. The Esk holds many delights; the valley road between Stokesley and Whitby crosses and re-crosses it many times. Rail travellers follow its course more closely between Middlesbrough and Whitby. But the best way to see Esk Dale is on foot. The Esk Valley Walk is a waymarked route, from Castleton to the golden coast at Whitby.

Unmissable attractions

Admire the fantastic views from Roseberry Topping...explore the many twists and turns of Whitby's bustling historic streets...visit the fascinating Moors Centre near Danby and discover what makes the North York Moors such a special place...cycle along the minor roads between Castleton, Danby and Lealholm in the Esk Valley...visit Egton Bridge in August and experience the famous Gooseberry Show...drive the high road over Castleton Rigg and enjoy moorland scenery at its best...admire the gleaming old locomotives getting up steam at Grosmont Station...relish the wooded surroundings of Gisborough Hall...get some sea air at Runswick – one of the loveliest sandy bays on the Yorkshire Coast.

1

1 Roseberry Topping
The distinctive shape of Roseberry Topping, seen here looming up out of the mist, gained its distinctive profile after intensive ironstone mining caused a huge landslip in 1921.

2 Whitby
Perched high on the clifftop east of Whitby are the magnificent ruins of St Hilda's Abbey.

3 Sandsend
This pretty village is set against a backdrop of cliffs at the northern end of a long arc of sandy beach.

31

CASTLETON

The castle is long gone from Castleton; only the name and a mound to the north of the village remain – unsentimentally, a lot of the stone from the ruined castle was probably recycled and used to build Danby Castle. Castleton used to have regular markets and a goods yard on the railway; the markets have gone, but the village still has its passenger station on the Esk Valley railway line.

Insight

MOORLAND 'INTAKES'

You'll probably notice a sudden dramatic contrast where the fields stop and open moorland begins, showing that the fields higher up the valley sides are 'intakes' – land 'taken in' from the moorland above. At the head of several moorland valleys are ruined farmsteads, which were abandoned when the living became too precarious. Here you will often see unmanaged grassy pasture reverting back to heather and bracken.

The River Esk, which rises at Esklets in Westerdale to the south, is joined at Castleton by a tributary, Commondale Beck. To the north of the village is an expanse of moorland, but the landscape is very different from that of the south, with a selection of minor roads, tracks and footpaths exploring a landscape of great variety. Two routes 'take the high road' over Castleton Rigg, enjoying panoramic views down into Westerdale and Danby Dale, and on to Ralph Cross (used as the National Park emblem) and the head of beautiful Rosedale. This is moorland scenery at its best; valley bottoms divided up into neat fields by drystone walls, the pattern interrupted by little copses.

You would probably hesitate to call Commondale, northwest of Castleton on the Esk Valley line, one of the prettier villages on the moors. This scattering of houses and farms occupies a hillside overlooking Commondale Moor. The village's most striking aspect

DANBY

is the use of brick, as much as stone, as a building material – the diminutive brick-built Church of St Peter, in particular, stands out like the proverbial sore thumb. The reason is very simple: until the 1950s Commondale had its own brickworks here, and bricks and tiles form vital decorative elements in a number of houses throughout the village, and on the façade of the old Co-op shop.

The village name was once written as 'Colmandale'. It is said that Colman, Bishop of Lindisfarne, stopped off here on his travels to Whitby Abbey.

DANBY

The pretty village of Danby lies on a crossroads; blink and you've missed it. But it was to this little village that John Atkinson came, at the age of 36, as minister of the parish. He was Essex-born and until the end of his long life retained the natural curiosity of the newcomer. One of his major passions was prehistory, and the moors – with their burial

Activity

CYCLING IN THE ESK VALLEY
The minor roads between Castleton, Danby and Lealholm in the Esk Valley are ideal for cycling as they are quiet and the valley floor level. With a little help from an OS Landranger map, it is possible to avoid most of the steep gradients on the roads out of the valley.

mounds, standing stones and moorland wayside crosses – provided much to excite his inquiring mind. He died in 1900, and is buried in the churchyard.

There are a number of interesting features in the immediate vicinity, and the easiest way to see them is to park at the National Park's Visitor Centre, just half a mile (800m) from the village on the road to Lealholm. The Moors Centre represents the public face of the National Park. Here you can discover what makes the North York Moors so special and the unique

35

habitats that the moors supports. The building that houses the Moors Centre was once a shooting lodge for the Dawnay family, who bought the Manor of Danby in 1656; it now hosts exhibitions and a wide variety of events, including guided walks. The evolution of the moorland landscape is explained, and those whose needs extend no further than a mug of tea and a slice of cake are equally well catered for. The Moors Centre sits in 13 acres (5.2ha) of land, close to the Esk, a lovely spot to enjoy a picnic or a stroll along the riverside. A number of waymarked walks explore the immediate environs; longer walks start from the car park.

Just a little way downstream is the intriguingly named Duck Bridge. This superb late 14th-century example of an arched packhorse bridge is a tangible reminder of a time when sturdy ponies, laden down with twin pannier bags, were the main means by which goods and sundries were transported between towns and villages.

The packhorse trail leads towards Danby Castle, once a fortified house of distinction, though most of the medieval stonework has since been incorporated into a farmhouse; there is only limited public access. The castle, built in the 14th century, was once the home of Catherine Parr, the sixth wife of Henry VIII, who fared better than his other wives and, indeed, survived him. Past Danby Castle Farm the road goes through a minor valley; Little Fryup Dale.

EGTON BRIDGE

Egton and Egton Bridge are two villages separated by both the River Esk and a steep descent. Egton has nothing to do with eggs; it appeared in the Domesday Book as Egetune, meaning 'the town of the oak trees'. The oaks are gone, as are the annual hiring fairs, when farmers would look to employ farm labourers for the forthcoming year. Even the weekly markets, for which the village was granted a charter by William

EGTON BRIDGE

of Orange, are no longer held in the village's broad street. But the village is important as the venue, every August, for one of the area's largest agricultural shows.

A new bridge, built in 1993, spans the River Esk at Egton Bridge. The stone arch replaces an ugly metal structure that was itself merely a replacement for the original bridge, which was swept away in floods in the 1930s.

Egton Bridge was the birthplace in 1599 of Father Nicholas Postgate, who ministered to his Catholic flock at much danger to himself. For the 'crime' of baptising a child into the Catholic faith, Father Postgate was sent for trial at York. He was found guilty and in 1678 was subjected – he was in his 80s – to the ultimate punishment of being hanged, drawn and quartered. In remaining staunchly Roman Catholic, Egton Bridge became known as 'the village missed by the Reformation'. The Catholic Church of St Hedda contains relics of Father Postgate's ministry. Half-way up the hill to Egton is a house with a tiny chapel hidden in the roof, reached by a secret passage. The room was discovered 150 years after Postgate's death, since when the house has been known as the Mass House.

Every year, in August, the famous Egton Bridge Gooseberry Show is held. You will have to be a spectator rather than a competitor – at least until you are voted in as a member of the Old Gooseberry Society, founded in 1800. Size, not taste, is what matters here.

Ramblers alight at Egton Bridge, a stop on the Middlesbrough to Whitby line, and walk along the Esk Valley to Lealholm to catch the next train home.

GLAISDALE

This village is a straggle of houses clinging to the hillside overlooking the River Esk. Ironstone was worked here. However, the Glaisdale mines were never as productive as those of nearby Rosedale.

Visit

RIVER CROSSINGS

Beggar's Bridge at Glaisdale, built in 1619, is now used by walkers; cars cross by a metal bridge, while trains on the scenic Esk Valley line pass almost overhead on a viaduct. Here, within the space of a few yards, much of the transport history of the last few centuries is represented.

The valley is steep-sided here, and even with the benefit of hairpin bends motorists have to negotiate the 1-in-3 gradient of Limber Hill on their way up to Egton with care. The area is criss-crossed with old tracks – a relic of a time when Glaisdale was an important trading centre. Through East Arncliff Wood the route is still marked by a line of causeway stones.

A number of these paths converge on Beggar's Bridge, a packhorse bridge with a romantic story. It was not easy to cross the Esk at the time when Tom Ferris was courting a local lass who lived on the opposite side of the river. If Tom was not actually a beggar, he was certainly a man of few means. He hoped to win the hand of his beloved by bettering his position, so he enlisted on a ship that was setting out from Whitby to fight against the Spanish Armada, or, as some say, as a privateer.

When he tried to say farewell to the lady, however, he was thwarted by the River Esk in spate. He sought fame and fortune, and became a very successful merchant and Lord Mayor of Hull. Yet he never forgot Glaisdale, and erected the splendid arch of Beggar's Bridge so that no other young lovers should be needlessly parted.

GREAT AYTON

Great Ayton is bisected by the River Leven, whose clear waters seem almost to deny that the industrial heartland of Middlesbrough is just a short drive away. Behind Great Ayton is the famous profile of Roseberry

GROSMONT STATION

Topping (1,056 feet/322m), the conical peak, a distinctive landmark for miles around.

Great Ayton has two churches that lie almost side by side. All Saints' Church is a delightful building dating back to the 12th century, though additions have been made in every succeeding century. The original tower was demolished in 1880. The interior is quite simple, with walls of rough-hewn stone, and enough original architectural detail to keep most lovers of old churches engrossed for a good while.

The population of Great Ayton grew to the point where the congregation could no longer squeeze into this atmospheric building. Christ Church was consecrated as the new parish church in 1877; fortunately the old church escaped the fate of so many redundant churches, and is now open to the public during the summer months. James Cook's mother and five of his brothers and sisters are buried in churchyard.

Visit

POSTGATE SCHOOL

Founded in 1704, the school in Great Ayton was designed to take eight poor boys of the town, but was soon accommodating up to 30 boys and girls. The school fees for the young James Cook were paid for by the lord of the manor, Thomas Skottowe, who employed Cook's father. The school is now home to the fascinating Captain Cook Schoolroom Museum.

GROSMONT

Built largely to house those who worked on the Pickering–Whitby railway line that splits the village in two, Grosmont was originally, and unimaginatively, called 'Tunnel'. With its terraced houses and mining spoil, Grosmont presents a more industrial face to the world than the other villages of the Esk Valley. Indeed, it was while excavating the Pickering-to-Whitby line, in 1835, that the richest ironstone deposits were first discovered. Once completed, the

Insight

THE RAIL TRAIL

The Rail Trail extends from Grosmont to Goathland, so it can be combined with a trip along this most scenic of railway lines (the Rail Trail booklet suggests the train journey to Goathland followed by a walk back to Grosmont). The 3-mile (4.8km) footpath follows the route of the original section of line between the two villages, via Beck Hole, as laid in 1836.

railway was a convenient method of ironstone delivery to ships in Whitby harbour. By the middle of the 19th century, Grosmont was a major supplier of ironstone to the ironmasters' furnaces on the Rivers Tyne and Tees.

The name 'Grosmont' recalls the 13th-century Grandmontine Priory, which was founded here by French monks. The priory is long gone, its place taken by Priory Farm and its stonework salvaged for reuse in secular buildings.

The Pickering–Whitby line was built in 1836 after consulting with George Stephenson, who came to the project straight from the triumphant success of his Stockton–Darlington railway. The line was closed, controversially, in 1965 by Beeching's infamous axe. It was reborn eight years later, thanks to massive support by railway enthusiasts, as the North Yorkshire Moors Railway, a recreational line manned by volunteers. There is nothing amateurish about the enterprise, though, for they maintain a regular timetable, come rain, shine, and even leaves on the line.

Railway buffs can spend some time admiring the gleaming old locomotives at Grosmont station, which has been convincingly restored to how it may it probably looked a century ago; there is also public access to the engine sheds.

Grosmont is the northern terminus of the railway, offering connections with main line services on the Esk Valley line between

PLATFORM 2

Brooke Bond Tea

NYMR WIN

ARO SPECIALISED LUBRICATION

ZEBRITE GRATE POLISH

CROSMONT

GROSMONT STATION

Middlesbrough and Whitby. It is a junction of roads and rivers, too, with the Murk Esk draining into the Esk.

GUISBOROUGH

Guisborough's broad main street and cobbled verges indicate that markets have been held here for centuries. The old market cross is topped by a sundial. Today the market traders put up their stalls on Thursdays and Saturdays, drawing their customers from many of the villages on the edge of the moors.

Like its close neighbour, Stokesley, the town's status has changed in recent years. Until the boundary changes of 1974, Guisborough was the capital town of the Cleveland district, which formed part of the North Riding of Yorkshire. Those reorganisations shifted the town into the county of Cleveland, but it is now back in North Yorkshire. Beyond the main street and the market cross is the largely 15th-century Church of St Nicholas, where a cenotaph reinforces the links between the local de Bruce family and the Bruces of Scotland. Robert the Bruce's grandfather is buried near by at Gisborough Priory.

The huge east window of the ruined Augustinian priory still stands to its full height of nearly 71 feet (20m), gazing out across farmland. To wander around the evocative ruins is to escape the bustle of Guisborough's busy streets. The priory was built in the early 14th century by Robert de Brus, who was related to the Scottish king, Robert the Bruce. In their contemplation of the life to come, the monks did not neglect to lay up their treasures on earth, and by the time of the Dissolution of the Monasteries they had become one of the richest communities in the north.

Nearby you'll find Gisborough Hall, now a luxury hotel, sits in beautiful wooded surroundings. The original hall was built by Sir Thomas Challoner, whose son began the mining of alum on the moors in about 1600. The industry proved to

LITTLE FRYUP DALE

be vital to the moorland economy for the following three centuries. Challoner stole the secrets of alum mining and processing from the Pope, no less, who had enjoyed a near-monopoly in the alum industry. He even persuaded some of the Pope's miners to accompany him back to England to begin alum mining on the moors. For this impertinence the Challoner family was excommunicated from the Catholic Church.

Just a mile (1.6km) out of town, on the A173 in the direction of Skelton, is Tocketts Mill. The water of Tocketts Beck still turns the waterwheel of this fine old flour-mill, and on certain milling days the building is open to the public.

KETTLENESS & GOLDSBOROUGH

Travellers on the A174 between Staithes and Whitby are seldom tempted to take one of the roads to the left, before they arrive in the roadside village of Lythe. The signpost indicates Goldsborough and Kettleness, a pair of hamlets whose history is by no means as tranquil as they appear today.

The handful of houses clustered together in Kettleness look as if they could fall off the cliff top at any minute. That's precisely what happened in 1829, when a landslip devastated the entire community. Fortunately, the villagers had enough warning of the impending disaster to vacate their homes and businesses and were rescued by a ship waiting for them offshore. But you may wonder, why bother to rebuild the village on such an exposed site? The answer can be found by taking a path down on to Kettleness Point, a barren and rocky promontory. Here are the remains of productive alum mines where alum was shovelled out of the cliffs.

How precarious a living alum mining provided can be appreciated by the fact that the foundations of a large number of the mining buildings end suddenly at the cliff edge. The folk of Kettleness lost their

KETTLENESS

livelihood, and their village, in the landslip of 1829; however, mining and processing of alum was fully operational again within five years. Alum was valued for its ability to fix dyes by the textile industries; other uses included applications in leather tanning, and the manufacture of candles and parchment.

Today, Kettleness Point is a dramatic moonscape, offering nesting sites for thousands of seabirds and, to the north, a view of Runswick Bay. The promontory forms part of the Heritage Coast, a sort of linear national park, which aims to preserve undeveloped coastlines with some of the most spectacular scenery along the east coast. Special protection is now given to the 36-mile (57.6km) stretch of superb coastline that lies between Saltburn and Scalby Ness, on the outskirts of Scarborough.

Goldsborough, half a mile (800m) inland, was the site of a 4th-century Roman signal station. The Roman road commonly known as

Wade's Causeway was probably built to link the settlement at Malton with the signal stations dotted at regular intervals along the coast. All that remains to be seen on the site are some grassy earthworks, sited 220 yards (200m) from the road linking Kettleness and Goldsborough. Excavations early in the 20th century produced a number of very interesting Roman finds, which suggested that the signal station might have ended its days by being suddenly ransacked. Near by you'll find a modern coastguard station.

The giant, Wade, whose moorland exploits are famous, is, according to legend, buried at Goldsborough. Two standing stones – one by Goldsborough Lane, the other adjacent to the A174 at East Barnby – are known as Wade's Stones and are said to mark the position of his head and feet. The stones are, however, more than half a mile (800m) apart, which would have made him stand out even at a giants' convention.

KILDALE

This little moorland village has a small station on the Esk Valley line between Middlesbrough and Whitby. Completed in 1865, the Esk Valley line had to make 17 river crossings between the stations at Kildale and Grosmont. It is still a valued amenity for locals and visitors.

St Cuthbert's Church is reached via a footbridge over the railway. A hoard of important Viking relics, including battle axes and swords, was discovered here in 1868 when the church was renovated. These finds show that Kildale was once an ancient settlement, a notion reinforced by earthworks and other finds in the area. A mound, cut into by the railway line, is now the only clue that Kildale once had a motte-and-bailey castle. This was one of the many strongholds owned by the Percy family, whose name is kept alive by names such as Percy Cross and Percy Rigg, high on the moors.

The Cleveland Way drops down briefly from the moors, to pass through Kildale. If you walk the route going north you will arrive on the breezy heights of Easby Moor where a monument, built in 1827, commemorates the life and exploits of Captain James Cook. From here you can enjoy views down over Great Ayton, where the young James Cook spent his formative years.

Kildale's rights of way were taken from an old map that marked only three, so there are few of the field paths that typify nearby villages. The road between Kildale and Westerdale offers splendid moorland scenery, and the watersplash over Baysdale Beck is a popular spot for a picnic on a summer's day.

LEALHOLM

The lovely River Esk runs through the narrow, wooded confines of Crunkly Gill, one of the many ancient gorges carved by Ice Age meltwaters, before flowing through Lealholm's grassy banks. This attractive little village, which sits astride a bend in the river, acts as a

LEALHOLM

magnet for visitors. Lealholm was a favourite place, too, for Canon Atkinson, Danby's vicar, who wrote lyrically about the village in his book, called *Forty Years in a Moorland Parish*, 'Elsewhere you must go in search of beautiful views; here they offer themselves to be looked at.'

The river is spanned by a fine, well-proportioned bridge of peach-coloured stone; just a few yards away is a line of ancient stepping stones that seem to have an irresistible attraction for small children. Beyond the bridge is the Board Inn, offering various refreshments and another vantage point from which to gaze down over the Esk.

Lealholm boasts no grand buildings of great note; visitors come here largely because the green is common land where they can roam at will and spread a picnic rug. On a sunny summer's day the river bank is a relaxing spot; greedy mallard ducks will eagerly dispose of any leftover sandwiches. Tea rooms and craft shops complete the picture. The National Park Authority has bowed to visitor pressure by providing a car park.

Lealholm can be grouped with other beauty spots, such as Goathland, Hutton-le-Hole and Thornton-le-Dale, as places best avoided on sunny Bank Holidays, unless you love crowds. Apart from that caveat, it's a delightful place.

ROSEBERRY TOPPING

Roseberry Topping, which lies just to the north of Great Ayton, is Cleveland's very own 'Matterhorn'. Its height, just 1,056 feet (322m), hardly qualifies it as a major peak, yet it is a prominent landmark for miles around, standing aloof from the surrounding Cleveland Hills.

To see Roseberry Topping as nature intended, as an almost symmetrical cone, you will have to look at old prints. As soon as its mineral wealth was realised, it was exploited for its alum, iron-ore, jet and roadstone. So heavily was it mined and quarried that a great chunk of the hill fell away in a landslip, making the residents of the nearby village of Newton under Roseberry fear for their lives.

This landslip created the distinctive profile we see today. Climb to the top, and to the northwest is the industrial heartland of Middlesbrough, its urban sprawl creeping inexorably outwards; to the south are magnificent panoramic views across the moors.

Roseberry Topping's prominence has made it an important landmark for more than a millennia. There is some evidence that it was even an object of veneration. 'Roseberry' is a corruption of the old Viking name, 'Othenesberg' (Odin's Hill), indicating it was probably sacred to the Danish god of creation. 'Topping', also of Scandinavian origin, means a peak. Several 17th-century references have it as 'Osbury Toppyne', at a time when it was one of the many beacon hills on which fires were built – to be set alight if the Spanish Armada were sighted at sea.

RUNSWICK BAY

A long arc of sandy beach extends south from the houses of Runswick, to form one of the loveliest bays on the Yorkshire coast. There is plenty of shelter from blustery winds and high seas; over the centuries many a ship's captain has been relieved to find safe harbour here.

The cliffs that protect the bay take a battering each winter; whole chunks can disappear in a storm. Since medieval times the coastline continues to change dramatically, with villages creeping ever closer to the shore, and many coastal villages sliding into the sea. You only have to look at old maps to realise that the 'lost' villages of Yorkshire's coast can be counted in scores.

The village of Runswick fell into the sea in 1682. Fortunately no lives were lost as all the villagers were evacuated in time. Today, Runswick comprises a pleasing collection of small red-roofed cottages, clinging limpet-like to the cliff and connected by a series of steps and alleyways.

RUNSWICK BAY

The sheltering bay, good soil and southerly aspect make Runswick a suntrap; in spring and summer the little terraced gardens make a pretty scene. The attractive whitewashed house on the headland was the coastguard's cottage.

A few fishing cobles are still lined up above the high watermark, though today your neighbour is more likely to be a holiday-maker than a fisherman. The lifeboat is always at the ready, however; ships can still be caught out by sudden changes in the weather. In 1901 a storm blew up while most of the fishing boats were at sea. The village women launched the lifeboat and saved many lives.

SANDSEND

The approach to Sandsend village along the A174 is steeply downhill from Lythe; views open up of a long sandy beach and, in the distance, Whitby Abbey dominates the horizon. Here is a place name that, for once, doesn't require interpretation. The village marks the northern end of

Visit

LEWIS CARROLL

It was while strolling along the fine, sandy beach at Sandsend that Lewis Carroll first had the idea for his surreal poem about the *Walrus and the Carpenter*. If you fancy it, you can follow in his footsteps; at low tide it is a lovely walk of about 2.5 miles (4km) along the beach to Whitby.

a sandy beach, one of the best on Yorkshire's coast, stretching down as far as Whitby harbour.

The village has been an industrious hive of activity for centuries; the Romans had a cement works here. More recently the bare outcrop of Sandsend Ness was mined for alum and it is still bare today, because of the heaps of mining waste. Remarkably, these mines were worked steadily for 250 years. When Yorkshire's coastal area had its railway, Sandsend was overlooked by a long viaduct, raised high above the red-tiled rooftops on

65

tall pillars. Both the railway and the viaduct disappeared in the 1960s: more's the pity, many may think.

Today, Sandsend is a more peaceful spot, sheltered from the from the rough battering of north winds and fiercesome seas by Sandsend Ness. Mickleby Beck and East Row Beck reach to the sea at Sandsend a mere 97 feet (30m) apart; instead of staring out to sea most of the cottages are neatly clustered either side of their banks. Several paths accompany both of these valleys into lovely Mulgrave Woods, which you'll find is a traditional broadleaved woodland. On the narrow ridge between these valleys is Georgian Mulgrave Castle. Guests at the castle included William Wordsworth and Charles Dickens; both wrote about the superb views. In the grounds are the evocative, ivy-clad ruins of a much earlier castle, dating from the 13th century.

STAITHES

It is easy to miss the Staithes turning off the main A174 coast road. Nor is the first sight of the village very promising. You have to drive half a mile (800m), park in the pay-and-display car park and proceed on foot if you want to see why Staithes is so special.

This perfectly preserved Yorkshire fishing villages is divided into two by Cowbar Beck and the steep-sided gorge through which it runs. For centuries the people of Staithes have had to cope with the twin problems of an inhospitable site and the ravages of the North Sea. They have made their living from the sea, while always taking care to respect its awesome power.

Activity

VIEWPOINTS ABOVE STAITHES

A walk of less than an hour from the village of Staithes will offer a variety of viewpoints, looking down on the random patchwork of red-tiled roofs from the cliff tops – known as Cowbar Nab and Old Nab – on either side of the gorge, connected by the arch of a footbridge.

The Staithes we see today is a village that would be immediately familiar to the young James Cook, who spent an impatient 18 months working at the counter of a draper's shop in the village before realising his ambition to go to sea. The whitewashed houses, pantiled roofs, fishing cobles and lobster pots would make him feel at home.

It may seem that time has stood still here, but the battering from the sea has been relentless. Despite the shelter given by its steep cliffs, Staithes has lost many buildings to its stormy seas. The little draper's shop was washed away; a house near the Cod and Lobster pub bears a commemorative plaque but has been rebuilt since James Cook lived and worked here. The pub itself backs on to the harbour wall and has suffered more than its fair share of storm damage, having been rebuilt three times – the last occasion being as recently as 1953.

On a sunny summer's day it is hard to imagine such destruction.

You would have to make your visit in winter, when a strong northeasterly gale is blowing, and the waves are hammering against the harbour wall, to understand why the people of Staithes have earned a reputation for self-reliance. To have maintained a viable community here, despite the drawbacks, is remarkable.

Fishing has long provided a living, albeit a precarious one, for the men of Staithes. The little harbour, and the mouth of Cowbar Beck, are still full of the traditional fishing cobles – whose slightly upturned prows betray their Nordic origins. But today they go to sea mainly for crabs and lobsters; you can buy them freshly caught in the village.

Painters and photographers are attracted in droves to the village. There are echoes of some of the picturesque fishing villages of Cornwall, but few communities in the country can boast a more extraordinary setting than Staithes. The village used to have a railway station; both station and line are gone, leaving just the trackbed and the stanchions of the old viaduct over the gorge as reminders of the scenic line that ran from Saltburn to Scarborough.

To the north of Staithes are Boulby Cliffs. At more than 650 feet (200m) they are the highest, if not the most dramatic, on England's east coast and offer excellent views. Close by is the Boulby Potash Mine, the deepest mine in Europe. The extent of the mining operation here can be gauged by the fact that tunnels extend almost 3 miles (4.8km) out under the sea.

WHITBY

Those who take a leisurely stroll along the pleasant harbour front may be forgiven for thinking of Whitby as just another resort devoted to the arcane delights of bingo, amusement arcades, candyfloss and 'Kiss Me Quick' hats. But Whitby has a great deal more to offer, enough to keep the most demanding visitor interested

Insight

A MAJOR FISHING PORT

Despite being popular with, photograhers and artists, sleepy Staithes has known busier days. The harbour is protected by the shaley cliff of Cowbar Nab and during the first half of the 19th century as many as 300 men went to sea in the distinctive fishing cobles, to net mostly cod, haddock and mackerel. These small craft, with a crew of three fishermen, were often accompanied by larger yawls.

Cobles (pronounced 'cobbles') are inspired, it is said, by Viking boats, they are clinker built – with the planks overlapping downwards – and are especially designed for launching from a beach. Fish were moved from the cobles into larger vessels for easier transport back to harbour. Fish was dispatched from Staithes all over the country; packhorses then carried some of each day's catch to the market at York.

Although the fishing business is not what it once was, you are still likely to see a number of smal boats bobbing in the water or leaning in the mud.

for some time. For it has a long, illustrious and genuine history as one of the country's most important seaports, and the town can claim associations with a remarkable variety of historical figures.

Whitby's setting itself is dramatic, with houses clinging on to the steep slopes on either side of the River Esk. A good overview of the town can be enjoyed from the elevated bridge that now carries through traffic on the A171 at a convenient distance from the town's narrow streets. From this vantage point you can see the Esk broaden into a large marina full of yachts. Beyond the swing bridge is the harbour, overlooked spectacularly on the southern flank by St Mary's Church and the ruined abbey – a landmark for miles around.

The scene is always one of bustle and activity. Whitby has thrived when other fishing towns and villages have declined, and new building projects emphasise that the town is looking to the future.

Whitby has always gazed out to sea. For centuries the town was isolated from the rest of the county by poor roads and the wild expanse of moorland that surround it on three sides. Yet by the 18th century it had risen to the status of a major port, with shipbuilding, fishing and whaling contributing to a maritime prosperity that lasted until well into the early years of the 20th century. The fine Georgian houses at the west end of the town, built by wealthy shipbuilders and fleet owners, attest to this success.

Elsewhere, more traditional cottages, whitewashed and with red-tiled roofs housed the fishermen. Space was at a premium, so their houses were built in close proximity, mostly up the steep inclines on the eastern side of the Esk. They are linked by ginnels and steps, which beg to be explored. Be sure to leave your car in one of the long-stay car parks near the marina; Whitby's narrow streets were definitely not built with motor traffic in mind.

Insight

WHITBY JET

Used to make jewellery since the Bronze Age, Whitby jet was popularised by Queen Victoria, who wore it during her many years of mourning for Prince Albert. Jet is fossilised wood, which turns from its natural brown colour to the deepest black ('jet-black', as we say) once it is polished, and Whitby proved a particularly fruitful site. This craft trade expanded as women took the royal lead and took to wearing jet ornaments. But their tastes were too fickle for the business to last indefinitely, and by the time of Victoria's death the demand for Whitby jet was much reduced. Today you can find original pieces of jewellery displayed in Whitby's Pannett Park Museum, and for sale in the town's antiques shops. Some new jet jewellery is being made too.

The town's large harbour is still at the heart of the town, though today there are more pleasure craft passing the breakwaters than fishing cobles. Whitby traditionally offered the only safe harbour between the rivers Tyne and Humber. The North Yorkshire coast is notoriously prone to storms, and many ships have been wrecked, unable to find sanctuary in time.

The town was prosperous during the 17th and 18th centuries with the mining and refining of alum – a vital ingredient in the dyeing of wool. Coal was brought here to fire the cauldrons that separated alum from rock, and stone was needed for building; this increase in trade required the building of a better harbour. In 1753 a company was set up in the town to undertake whaling expeditions, using the sturdy ships already being built here. The ships spent many weeks at sea in the distant, inhospitable waters of the Arctic. The trade was lucrative for those who survived; some ships, sadly, never returned. Records reveal that almost 3,000 whales were brought back to Whitby up to 1833. Seals, walruses and polar bears also featured in these hauls, and even unicorns, if the records are to be believed. They were more likely to have been narwhals, whose single 'horn' probably started the unicorn myth in the first place.

The whale blubber was rendered down on the quayside to make oil; the stench, by all accounts, was vile. Even the streetlamps of the town were lit with gas refined from whale oil. An arch formed from the jawbone of a whale looks down upon the harbour today.

Smaller boats sailed out of Whitby to net herring, and the fish market was one of the busiest. The men still fish, but on a much reduced scale; many of the boats that slip anchor today are carrying sea anglers and other visitors.

The town has a special place in ecclesiastical history. In the year AD 655 King Oswy of Northumbria celebrated a heady victory in battle by promising his daughter as a bride of Christ. He founded a monastery on Whitby's eastern cliff,

Insight

FRANK MEADOW SUTCLIFFE

Photographer Frank Meadow Sutcliffe's bread-and-butter work was portraiture. But his passion was the town and architecture of Whitby itself. He used a huge and cumbersome camera, which precluded any modern notion of candid photography, to photograph the town. He stage-managed his compositions (even paying some of his subjects to ensure co-operation) to produce lustrous images of gnarled old fishermen, street traders and grubby street urchins – with the tall-masted sailing ships and Whitby harbour as picturesque backdrops.

It isn't merely the patina of age that makes Sutcliffe's pictures so beguiling. All the characters he photographed may be long gone, but many of the locations can still be seen today. Despite the cars, the cafés and the candyfloss, there is a continuing thread that links the Whitby of today to the Whitby that Sutcliffe knew so well. At the Sutcliffe Gallery you can find framed prints of his evocative photographs, all taken from the negatives.

overlooking the town, much where the later abbey's ruins still stand today. The first abbess was Hilda, who presided over a community of nuns and monks. Her goodness and piety passed into legend, and she was recognised as a saint. In AD 664 the Synod of Whitby convened in the town to decide whether Northumbria should follow the Catholic or Celtic Christianity. In the event the Catholic Church triumphed.

The most notable member of this community was Caedmon, also known as the 'Father of English poetry'. A shy man, he preferred to keep his own company as a cowherd instead of singing with the choir. Caedmon had a dream in which an angel asked him to sing. When he awoke, he found that he was possessed of a beautiful voice. His poem, called *The Song of Creation,* is the earliest known poem written in English. A sandstone cross by St Mary's Church commemorates his life and carved panels illustrate some of the incidents in his life.

St Hilda's original abbey was destroyed by Viking raiders. The abbey that replaced it was begun in the 11th century and was rebuilt on several occasions, notably in the 13th and 14th centuries; this is what we can see today. This building, too, suffered damage, when in 1914 two German battleships shelled the town and inadvertently hit the west front of Whitby Abbey.

Sharing the abbey's windswept site is St Mary's Church. It was built to serve the spiritual needs of village that grew up around the abbey. St Mary's still serves the congregations, although its parishioners have to tackle the famous 199 steps up to the church. Parts of the building date back to the 12th century; fortunately the fabric of the church suffered none of the indignities meted out to the abbey. Make sure to take a look inside; the interior was fitted out during the 18th century with wooden galleries, high-sided box-pews and a three-decker pulpit. The effect is quite startling, with a distinctly nautical feeling as if the craftsmen were more accustomed to fitting out ships.

At the bottom of Church Steps is the oldest part of Whitby town. Little fishermen's cottages huddle together as if to keep out the bitterly cold weather and harsh winds that blow off the sea. Narrow alleyways lead off from the tiny market square, and if those 199 steps have taken their toll enjoy a drink in one of the harbour-side pubs and watch the fishing boats and pleasure craft.

On Grape Lane, by the harbour, you will find the home of ship owner and Quaker, Captain John Walker, to whom the young James Cook was apprenticed in 1746, before achieving his dream and enlisting in the Royal Navy. Today the building houses the Captain Cook Memorial Museum, with room sets and interesting exhibits about his life.

Whitby Museum in Pannett Park, off St Hilda's Terract is also worth a visit. It provides fascinating exhibits of local fossils, plants and animals, as well as detailing the archaeology of the area. There are many models of ships and you can learn about the whaling fleet from Whitby and about Captain Cook – the museum has several of his manucripts. The collection reflects the far-flung journeys of Whitby sailors, with Japanese armour and a calabash from Cameroon.

Insight & Visit

DRACULA

Few church graveyards enjoy a more panoramic view than the one surrounding St Mary's Church. But if the wind is whipping around the gravestones, and the full moon is shrouded by clouds, it can have a rather more menacing atmosphere. Bram Stoker realised its dramatic potential and avid readers of his horror novel, *Dracula,* will recognise some of the settings from Whitby. Look out for the skull and crossbones gravestones near the topmost gate. These are said to have inspired the novel.

TOURIST INFORMATION CENTRES

Danby
The Moors Centre.
Tel: 01287 660654

Great Ayton
High Green Car Park.
Tel: 01642 722835 (Seasonal)

Guisborough
Priory Grounds, Church Street.
Tel: 01287 633801

Whitby
Langborne Road.
Tel: 01723 383636

PLACES OF INTEREST

Captain Cook and Staithes Heritage Centre
High Street, Staithes.
Tel: 01947 841454

Captain Cook Memorial Museum
Grape Lane, Whitby.
Tel: 01947 601900;
www.cookmuseumwhitby.co.uk

Captain Cook Schoolroom Museum
Great Ayton.
Tel: 01642 724296; www.
captaincookschoolroommuseum.co.uk

The Dracula Experience
9 Marine Parade,
Whitby.
Tel: 01947 601923

Gisborough Priory
Guisborough.
Tel: 01287 633801

Lifeboat Museum
Pier Road, Whitby.
Tel: 01947 602001

The Moors Centre
Lodge Lane, Danby.
Tel: 01439 772737 or
01287 660792;
www.nationalparks.gov.uk/
nym_core

Tocketts Watermill
On A173, 1 mile (1.6km) east of
Guisborough.

Tom Leonard Mining Museum
Skinningrove.
Tel: 01287 642877;
www.ironstonemuseum.co.uk

Victorian Jet Works
123B Church Street, Whitby.
Tel: 01947 821530;
www.whitbyjet.net

Whitby Abbey
East Cliff, Whitby.
Tel: 01947 603568
Whitby Museum and Art Gallery
Pannett Park, Whitby.
Tel: 01947 602908

SHOPPING
Guisborough
Open-air market, Thu and Sat.
Whitby
Open-air market, Tue and Sat.

LOCAL SPECIALITIES
Ceramics, Sculpture and Jewellery
Montage Studio Gallery,
12 Church Street, Castleton.
Tel: 01287 660159
Enamel
The Enamel Gallery,
128 Church Street, Whitby.
Tel: 01947 606216
Glass
Whitby Glass Studios,
9 Sandgate, Whitby.
Tel: 01947 603553;
www.whitbyglass.com

Paintings and Prints
John Freeman Studios,
9 Market Place, Whitby.
Tel: 01947 602799;
www.johnfreemanstudio.co.uk
Grosmont Gallery
Grosmont.
Tel: 01947 895007;
www.grosmontgallery.com
Whitby Jet
Watsons Jet Workshop,
Church Street, Whitby.
Tel: 01947 605320
Whitby Jet Heritage Centre,
Church Street, Whitby.
Tel: 01947 821530;
www.whitbyjet.net

PERFORMING ARTS
Glaisdale
Esk Valley Summer Theatre (seasonal).
Tel: 01947 897587
Whitby
Whitby Pavilion Theatre
West Cliff, Whitby.
Tel: 01947 604855 or 820625;
www.whitbypavilion.co.uk

SPORTS & ACTIVITIES
ANOLINO
Sea
Staithes & Whitby
Enquire at the harbour,
or contact the local TIC.

Fly
River Esk
Information on licences and permits
from main post offices. Fishing
locations from the Environment
Agency, Rivers House,
21 Park Square South, Leeds.
Tel: 0113 2440191
Scaling Dam Reservoir
Fishing lodge:
Tel: 01287 640540

BEACHES
Runswick Bay has a sandy beach with
easy access; a sandy beach stretches
from Whitby to Sandsend with car
parks and access points.

BOAT TRIPS
Whitby
Trips round the bay leave from the
West Pier.

CYCLE HIRE
Hawsker
(Whitby to Scarborough rail trail)
Trailways Cycle Hire,
The Old Railway Station,
Hawsker, near Whitby.
Tel: 01947 820207;
www.trailways.info

HORSE-RIDING
Lealholm
Hollin Hall Riding Centre,
Great Fryup Dale.
Tel: 01947 897470;
www.hollinequest.co.uk

Borrowby
Borrowby Equestrian Centre, High
Farm, Borrowby.
Tel: 01947 840134;
www.borrowbyequestriancentre.co.uk

LONG-DISTANCE FOOTPATHS & TRAILS

The Cleveland Way

A 110-mile (176km) walk from Helmsley to Filey Brigg.
www.clevelandway.gov.uk

The Esk Valley Walk

Begins at Castleton and follows the River Esk to Whitby.

WATERSPORTS

Scaling Dam Reservoir

Sailing, windsurfing.
Tel: 01287 640214

ANNUAL EVENTS & CUSTOMS

Castleton

Castleton Show, Sep.

Danby

Agricultural Show, mid-Aug.

Egton

Egton Show, late Aug.
Egton Bridge
Gooseberry Show, early Aug.

Kildale

Kildale Show, early Sep.

Lealholm

Lealholm Show, early Sep.

Whitby

Planting of the Penny Hedge, Ascension Eve, May.
Morris Dance Festival, Jun.
Blessing of Boats, mid-Jul.
Whitby Angling Festival, Jul.
Whitby Folk Festival, Aug.
Whitby Regatta, mid-Aug.

TEA ROOMS

Beck View Tea Room,
Lealholm, YO21 2AQ
Tel: 01947 897310
There are tables inside the cosy tea room and outside on the beck's bank. As well as good-value cream teas, regular visitors enjoy a good variety of home-made cakes, including the particularly scrumptious nut slice.

Elizabeth Botham & Sons
35/39 Skinner Street,
Whitby, YO21 3AH
Tel: 01947 602823
www.botham.co.uk
The tradition of fine baking, begun in 1865, is still going strong in this superior first-floor café on Whitby's West Cliff. Your problem will be what to choose – gingerbread with Wensleydale cheese, lemon buns, Yorkshire tea brack loaf, the cream tea, the salads, the sandwiches or baked potatoes.

Macdonald Gisborough Hall,
Whitby Lane, Guisborough, TS14 6PT
Tel: 0870 400 8191; www.macdonaldhotels.co.uk/gisborough
For a taste of luxury, in elegant surroundings, treat yourself at Gisborough Hall. As well as scones with jam and cream, there's the Gisborough Hall Tea, with smoked salmon and ham finger sandwiches, chocolate brownies and boiled fruit cake, as well as scones, or the Yorkshire Tea, where your scones and fruitcake are accompanied by Wensleydale cheese. Tea is served from midday to 6pm.

Stonehouse Bakery & Tea Shop,
3 Briar Hill Avenue, Danby, YO21 2LZ
Tel: 01287 660006
This traditional bakery produces fabulous bread, including sun-dried tomato and olive breads and ciabatta. They are used to make the range of sandwiches that available in the adjoining tea shop. Cakes, too, come from the bakery's ovens, and their scones are perfect with jam and cream.

DANBY CASTLE

Duke of Wellington Inn
Danby, YO21 2LY
Tel: 01287 660351
www.danby-dukeofwellington.co.uk

An attractive inn, in the scattered village of Danby with wide views of the village in its moorland setting. Inside, the décor is warm, welcoming and traditional, with local beers and a good selection of whiskies. The evening menu tends to be more adventurous than the lunchtime offerings.

The Royal Oak Hotel
125 High Street,
Great Ayton, TS9 6BW
Tel: 01642 722361
www.royaloak-hotel.co.uk

Located in the heart of the tranquil village of Great Ayton, you'll find the Royal Oak to be a traditional, relaxed pub. The beamed bar provides good local beer and hearty bar snacks, while the restaurant serves simple, robust and well-cooked food with a range of puddings, so leave room for one.

The Wheatsheaf Inn,
Egton, YO21 1TZ
Tel: 01947 895271

There's a plentiful supply of Yorkshire ales in the Wheatsheaf, including Black Sheep from Masham. The pub's exterior is unassuming, but inside, the main bar has low beams, dark walls and comfortable settles. There is much good pub food on offer, using local fish and other produce – the fish stew is recommended.

Western Moors

AMPLEFORTH

BILSDALE

BRANSDALE

CHRISTIAN CROSSES
   & MONKS

CLEVELAND WAY

COXWOLD

HAWNBY

HELMSLEY

KILBURN

OSMOTHERLEY

OSWALDKIRK

RIEVAULX ABBEY

STOKESLEY

SUTTON BANK

INTRODUCTION

The Western Moors include Helmsley, a handsome little market town and the administrative centre of the National Park. Near by you'll find the ruins of Rievaulx and Byland abbeys and the White Horse of Kilburn. The rolling Hambleton Hills and the bleaker Cleveland Hills provide a landscape of gorgeous heather moorland and pastoral dales, dotted with charming farmhouses and villages of red-tiled stone houses.

Unmissable attractions

There's no lack of things to enjoy here and Helmsley is an excellent base from which to explore the Western Moors...take a picnic to Chop Gate for fine views...walk the drove road called Westside Track near Cockayne...stroll on Rievaulx Terrace and view the fine abbey below...walk northwards from the car park at Sutton Bank along part (or all!) of the Cleveland Way for magnificent views...see the craftsmen carvers hard at work at the Mouseman Visitor Centre in Kilburn...follow the Mosaic Trail from Boltby... explore the ruins of Helmsley Castle...contemplate a monk's life in a cell at Mount Grace Priory...catch a concert in a remote country church during the Ryedale Festival...see Coxwold's superb octagonal church tower from the gardens of Shandy Hall.

1

1 Rievaulx Abbey

The atmospheric and evocative ruins of 13th-century Rievaulx Abbey, one of the great monastic houses of the north, are set in the tranquil wooded valley of the River Rye.

2 Hemlsley Castle

Little remains of Helmsley Castle's great East Tower, built in the 12th century by Robert de Roos. The castle was destroyed by Parliamentarians after a three-month siege in 1644.

3 Sutton Bank

The wonderful views from the vantage point of Sutton Bank, on the edge of the Hambleton Hills, take in the prominent landmark of Roulston Scar, wooded Hood Hill and the Vale of York.

AMPLEFORTH

Best known for its boys' public school and Benedictine monastery, Ampleforth is a linear village of handsome houses overlooking the Howardian Hills.

French monks, fleeing persecution in their homeland in 1793 during the course of the French Revolution, found spiritual sanctuary in England and patronage from the prominent Fairfax family, settling at Ampleforth in 1802. As theirs had been a teaching order, they built a school within the monastery. The oldest surviving school buildings date from 1861, while the monastery dates from 1894–98. But both establishments have been extended almost continuously up to the present day.

Just after the end of World War I, headmaster Father Paul Nevill, who was also the parish priest, commissioned Robert Thompson of Kilburn to make a wooden cross for the churchyard in the village. Father Nevill was so impressed by

Visit

BRIDESTONES

On top of Hasty Bank, the northern escarpment of the Cleveland Hills, are the Wainstones, the largest outcrop of rocks in the National Park, and a favourite with rock climbers. Another set of superb rocks can be found on Nab End Moor, in Bilsdale. These are just one of a number of rock formations on the moors that are known as the Bridestones. Others, the remains of ancient stone circles, can be found near Grosmont. The best-known Bridestones are in the hands of the National Trust on Bridestones Moor, and are most easily approached from the Dalby Forest Drive. Weathered into strange shapes, these rocks make a surreal, and unmissable, moorland landmark.

the woodcarver's craftsmanship that Thompson was asked to make furniture for the school. The library remains one of Robert Thompson's most ambitious commissions. The present abbey church is a new

BILSDALE

SUN INN

addition, built between 1922 and 1961 to a design by Sir Gilbert Scott; it too contains several very fine examples of woodwork and carvings by Robert Thompson.

Just southeast of Ampleforth is Gilling East, which has a 14th-century fortified tower house. Since early in the 20th century the building has been owned by Ampleforth College, and used as the college's preparatory school.

BILSDALE

The long valley of Bilsdale extends all the way along the B1257, from Helmsley in the south towards Stokesley in the north. The broad valley is farmed up to the moorland tops, as it was centuries ago by the monks of Rievaulx Abbey.

The monastic connection is recalled by names such as Crossholme and Low Crosses Farm. Scattered farmsteads punctuate the valley, but today the only village is tiny Chop Gate. Pronounce it 'Chop Yat' to sound like a local.

Visit

PICNIC SITES

Five miles (8km) north of Helmsley on the B1257, just before you enter Bilsdale, is Newgate Bank, a fine vantage point with a picnic site, from where you can enjoy views of Bilsdale and the Hambleton Hills. A footpath returns to Helmsley via Riccal Bank. At the northern end of Bilsdale is the village of Chop Gate, which also has a picnic site and a car park.

The River Seph is ever-present in the valley bottom; the B1257 accompanies it almost from its source to where it joins the River Rye to the north of Rievaulx. On the roadside about 8 miles (12.8km) north of Helmsley is the Sun Inn. Just yards away from the pub is a much earlier thatched building, of cruck-frame construction, that dates back to the 16th century. This was the original Sun Inn – also known as Spout House – which dispensed ale from first receiving its licence in

101

Visit

THE GILLAMOOR SUNDIAL

Gillamoor boasts a sundial of novel design in front of Dial House Farm; it was erected by public subscription in 1800. A central column is mounted on top of a stepped base. On top is a stone globe mounted on an inscribed cube, with a dial face on four of its sides.

1714 until 1914. When the licence transferred to the new Sun Inn, the older building fell into disrepair. The National Park Authority rescued and renovated this delightful example of vernacular architecture.

Now it is considered to be the finest example of a cruck-framed house in the National Park (not counting those in Ryedale Folk Museum) and one of the oldest. Visitors can take a look inside. The interior has been restored to how it might have looked more than three centuries ago. A witch post still stands near the inglenook fireplace,

to ward off the 'evil eye'. Up narrow stairs are tiny rooms, open to the thatch and fitted out with wooden box beds. Downstairs are the diminutive bar and cosy snugs of the original pub, and the beer cellar.

BRANSDALE

The unspoiled valley of Bransdale drives deep into the moors, but most visitors pass it by. Motorists leaving Helmsley along the A170 towards Kirkbymoorside should look out on the left for a signpost to Carlton (and Helmsley Youth Hostel). The road loops around Bransdale and then returns to the A170 about 5 miles (8km) further east at Kirkbymoorside.

Beyond the houses that comprises the village of Carlton, the views open up dramatically. To the left is unenclosed heather moorland; to the right the valley bottom is divided up by neat drystone walls either side of Hodge Beck. This pattern is punctuated by a handful of scattered farmsteads. The moors, with barely a tree to be seen, echo to the evocative calls of the curlew, red grouse and lapwing; sheep graze the grassy verges and wander idly across the road. Unenclosed for most of the way, the road heads north; look out on the left for examples of inscribed milestones.

The Church of St Nicholas sits on a hillock overlooking the valley. Though dating only from 1886, the building replaces a much earlier church. It is a typical moorland church, tiny and rather undemonstrative, but with a real sense of spirituality that grander churches so often lack. Inside, the barrelled roof is worth a look.

Flour was ground for centuries at Bransdale Mill (National Trust, but not open to the public), accessible, on foot only, from either side of the valley head. The present building, dating from 1811, was built by William Strickland and his son, Emmanuel, the vicar of Ingleby Greenhow. Stones inset into the mill walls are inscribed with

Activity

A CYCLE TOUR THROUGH BRANSDALE

The unclassified road which leaves the A170 at Helmsley and curves round in a loop through Bransdale before rejoining the A170 again at Kirkbymoorside is an ideal route for cyclists. Passing through the villages of Carlton, Cockayne and Gillamoor, the 12-mile (19km) tour offers wonderful moorland views with lonely farms and tumbling streams.

'improving' texts in Hebrew, Latin and Greek; evidence of the vicar's fine classical education.

The road then makes a broad sweep to the right, before continuing the circuit of Bransdale. Here sturdy farmsteads with fanciful names – Cow Sike, Toad Hole and Spout House – gaze down into the bottom of the valley. Before arriving in Kirkbymoorside, you have a chance to visit Gillamoor and Fadmoor, a pair of typical moorland villages barely half a mile (800m) apart.

BRANSDALE

The houses of both these pretty and unspoilt villages are grouped around their village greens, but Gillamoor has an extra surprise in store for the visitor. St Aidan's Church stands on its own at the end of the village; you are almost upon it before you see that it is sited on the edge of a steep precipice which commands breathtaking views across lower Farndale, the River Dove and on to the purple heather moors beyond.

CHRISTIAN CROSSES & MONKS

The life and landscape of the North York Moors have been shaped by a number of influences, but few have had a longer or more profound effect than the Christian faith. The moorland monasteries may be evocative ruins today, but in days gone by the influence of these communities extended far beyond the silence of their cloisters. For example, by the start of the 16th century about a third of the land within what is now the Peak District National Park was under the direct control of various monasteries.

The monks combined their religious devotions with remarkably successful forays into more secular activities. They may have chosen isolated sites on which to build their communities and churches, but they were not averse to comfort – even luxury. The religious buildings of the moors trace their origins back many centuries. A number of extant churches and abbeys pre-date the Norman invasion. Many more recent edifices are built on the foundations of much earlier buildings. The link with the past is everywhere.

At the dawning of the 7th century, these moors formed part of the Northumbrian Kingdom of Deira. King Edwin of Northumbria was saved from assassination by the intervention of Lilla, one of his ministers. Edwin is said to have marked Lilla's grave on Fylingdales Moor with a stone cross – the oldest of the famous moorland crosses. In AD 627 Edwin was converted to

Christianity by Paulinus, a Roman missionary. The first Christian communities in the area covered by this book were in Whitby (at that time known as Streanaeshalch) and Lastingham. In AD 654 St Cedd was given land at Lastingham to build a monastery. Just three years later Whitby Abbey was founded by Abbess Hilda, who presided over male and female devotees on this exposed cliff-top site.

Although the monasteries of Whitby and Lastingham were sacked by the Vikings, the seeds of Christianity proved to have been sown in fertile ground. By the end of the 10th century the Danish and Norwegian settlers had mostly been converted to the faith. St Gregory's Minster at Kirkdale is a fascinating pre-Norman church.

It was only after the Norman invasion, however, that the great monastic houses on the moors were founded. Benedictine monks returned to the site of St Hilda's monastery in Whitby and established

Insight

ENTREPRENEURIAL MONKS

The various monastic communities of the North York moors owned outlying farms – known as granges, which were often located many miles from the monasteries. The monks (their numbers augmented by lay brothers) devoted their talents to arable farming, animal husbandry and exploiting the uplands for their mineral wealth. The monks' entrepreneurial skills created international markets for their wares and, in many cases, immense wealth and power for the monasteries.

another five communities in the area. The Cistercian Order was created by French monks. Finding the Benedictine regime too ready to succumb to earthly temptations, they vowed to emphasise once again the virtues of hard work and austerity. In 1131 a band of monks from France crossed the Channel and were endowed with land in Ryedale on which to build a monastery.

The monks gave a French twist to the valley's name and called their community Rievaulx.

From small beginnings the Cistercian community prospered. By the time of the third abbot, St Aelred, the number of ordained monks – about 150 – was swelled by more than 600 lay brethren. Outlying farms, known as 'granges', were set up – often at some distance from the mother church. Contemplation and prayer played a great part in the monks' lives, but they worked hard on the land too.

The monks of Rievaulx developed the mining of ironstone that, many centuries on, would help to create the industrial wealth around the Tees and the Tyne. The upland moors provided grazing for huge flocks of sheep. The land (a gift from a local landowner) may have been poor for agriculture, but the monks successfully exploited it as grazing land. Wool from Rievaulx became renowned throughout Europe for its excellence.

The monks cleared forests to provide fuel for the iron furnaces. They drained land, built roads and spanned the River Rye and other rivers with sturdy bridges. They even built a system of canals to facilitate the transport of iron and stone. All this activity was in addition to the huge task, undertaken over a period of 60 years, of building Rievaulx Abbey; the impressive remains of the high church and monastic buildings still lift the spirits of visitors today.

The Carthusian Order was another to have had its origins in France. Mount Grace Priory, near Osmotherley, was founded in 1398; the ruins are believed to be the finest example of Carthusian building in the country.

Franciscan friars, who followed the strict teachings of St Francis, came to Scarborough. Their doctrine of absolute poverty provided a stark contrast to the business-like ethos and prosperity of the Carthusians. The Augustinian Canons built the splendid Gisborough Priory; visitors

Insight

ANCIENT WAYMARKERS

More than thirty moorland stone crosses still survive today; at one time there were many more. One of their functions was to define the far-flung boundaries of the sheep-grazing moors of the monasteries. But their religious symbolism is obvious, and many a lost and lonely traveller would have had his spirits lifted by the sight of a cross on the horizon. Crosses were often sited along old roads and many doubled as waymarkers. An interesting custom was for well-heeled travellers to leave coins on top of the crosses (many had a recess for this purpose) for the benefit of their needier brethren.

CLEVELAND WAY

When it was inaugurated in 1969 the Cleveland Way was only the second national trail in the country – coming just four years after Tom Stephenson's pioneering work in creating the Pennine Way. The name derives from the Cleveland Hills and is a little ambiguous, since for most of its 110-mile (176km) it lies inside the North York Moors National Park.

The walk, a roughly horseshoe-shaped route, breaks into two distinct sections. From the starting point at Helmsley, the route meanders through the moorland scenery of the Hambleton and Cleveland Hills. Walkers reach the highest point within the National Park when they traverse Urra Moor. Once the North Sea is sighted, at Saltburn, walkers follow the coastal path down to the finishing point at Filey Brigg. The walk can be divided up into sections that offer a single day's hike, each ending at a point where accommodation is available.

to the site can see the great arch of the east window that still stands.

Between 1536 and 1540, after his break with Rome, Henry VIII ordered the closure of the abbeys and Dissolution of Monasteries, bringing to an end their huge and wide-ranging influence.

ATON BANKS WOOD

Activity

THE MISSING LINK

An extra section of the Cleveland Way, known as the Missing Link, has been developed to take walkers in a complete loop from Scarborough back to Helmsley. This circular walk is about 180 miles (288km) long, and means that walkers can now start and finish at any convenient point on the route.

COXWOLD

Coxwold, about 3 miles (5km) south of Kilburn, has a 15th-century village church, with a distinctive eight-sided tower, overlooking the handsome houses lining the broad main street, which include almshouses dating back to the reign of Charles II.

Fifteenth-century Shandy Hall, lies opposite to the church, and was once the home of Laurence Sterne (1713–68). As a writer Sterne was a relatively late developer, not picking up his quill until the ripe age of 46. The publication of his picaresque novel, *The Life and Opinions of Tristram Shandy, Gentleman*, coincided with his becoming the vicar of Coxwold. However, Sterne's spiritual ambitions had to compete with his love of gambling, horse racing and cock fighting. On one occasion, while vicar of Stillington, near York, he left his congregation while he went after partridges with a shotgun. Literary success was immediate, and Sterne was able to indulge his taste for high living. He contracted pleurisy and died in 1768. His skull is buried in Coxwold churchyard. Dilapidated Shandy Hall was renovated in the 1960s, filled with manuscripts and first editions and opened to the public.

To the south is Newburgh Priory, which was designed and built as an Augustinian house in 1145. After the Dissolution of Monasteries, Henry VIII rewarded his chaplain, Anthony Bellasis, by giving him the building. He, and the owners who followed him, transformed the priory into a fine country house.

SHANDY HALL

The beautiful setting of Byland Abbey (English Heritage) wasn't the first site chosen by the band of Cistercian monks who came here from France. They had settled briefly near Old Byland, but it was reckoned to be unsuitable because the monks were confused by hearing the bells of nearby Rievaulx Abbey. Finally, in 1177, work began on Byland Abbey.

Insight

A FASTIDIOUS VICAR

Charles Norris Gray was vicar of Helmsley from 1870 to the onset of World War I, and had a reputation as a doughty fighter for his chosen causes, which included the state of the drains, the dangers of wearing tight corsets and the lack of cleanliness among the lower orders. Who knows the state to which Helmsley might have degenerated without such a strong hand on the tiller? The vicarage was one of the many buildings whose restoration Gray supervised; today the building is the administrative centre of the National Park.

Not as complete now as either Rievaulx or Fountains Abbeys, its church was nevertheless larger than either. The dramatic west façade, with its 26-foot (8m) diameter window, still stands to its full height, and gives an impression of just how huge the nave used to be.

HAWNBY

The remote village of Hawnby is best approached from the south. A long view opens up, with the red-roofed houses of the village appearing to cling to a ledge on the flank of Hawnby Hill. This sunny situation encourages residents to create colourful terraced gardens. To the right are the equally rounded contours of Easterside Hill. The environs of Hawnby comprise one of the loveliest landscapes in the National Park and it is well worth leaving the car and exploring on foot. Winding roads and tracks offer superb views at every turn. This gently undulating moorland landscape left an impression on John Wesley, the founder of Methodist Church, who came here to preach in 1757: 'I rode through one of the pleasantest parts of England to Hawnby'. John Wesley's inspirational sermons preached in Hawnby gained it a reputation as a stronghold of Methodism.

He had come from Osmotherley, across the expanse of Snilesworth Moor, so it would have been a relief to arrive in the sheltered, wooded valley of the River Rye. The road between Hawnby and Osmotherley has a rather better surface than in Wesley's day, but it still twists and turns through beautiful countryside.

The little Church of All Saints, in a riverside setting near the bridge, has features which date to the 12th century. Beyond the church is Arden Hall (not open), almost hidden in the woods. It was built on the site of a 12th-century Benedictine nunnery, the hall is the seat of the Earls of Mexborough. Mary, Queen of Scots, stayed here on her long road to the executioner's axe.

HELMSLEY

The handsome market town of Helmsley is where the National Park Authority has its administrative headquarters. Here too is a well-stocked Tourist Information Centre, in the castle, where visitors can browse for maps, informative books and brochures about the area.

It may be only the size of a large village, but Helmsley has the purposeful, bustling, reassuring air of a county town. It is especially busy on Friday, which is market day. The old market cross on its stepped base is still in place, though the square is dominated by a more elaborate monument, designed by Sir Gilbert Scott to commemorate the second Lord Feversham.

A number of roads converge here; at one time this was an important halt on stagecoach routes. A regular service ran to London from the Black Swan Inn, which still has a large wooden swan in place of an inn sign. These days more adventurous souls arrive with walking boots,

cagoules and rucksacks, for Helmsley is the starting point of the Cleveland Way, a 110-mile (176km) national trail that takes off across the moors before following the coastal path down to Filey. Cleveland wayfarers should follow the 'acorn' signs up Castlegate, to get an excellent view of the castle standing 'head and shoulders' above the little town, before descending into Rye Dale and the ruins of Rievaulx Abbey.

As is the case with many other North Yorkshire towns, behind Helmsley's prosperity is a castle and a prominent family. Of Walter l'Espec's first castle no traces now remain; the fortification we see today dates back to the 12th century. Robert de Roos was rewarded for his part in the Norman invasion by being given the manor of Helmsley. The de Roos family owned the castle until it was sold to Sir Charles Duncombe. Now cared for by English Heritage.

The castle was built for defence rather than show, yet it didn't witness any military action until the Civil War. It was here that the troops of Colonel Jordan Crossland, a loyal supporter of Charles I, were besieged by the Parliamentarian army of Sir Thomas Fairfax, which numbered a thousand troops. The siege, against what was regarded as one of the country's most impregnable fortresses, lasted three months. It might have lasted longer, but Royalist reinforcements were intercepted, and provisions

Insight

DAYS GONE BY

Helmsley was a major stopping point on stagecoach routes in days gone by and it is easy to imagine weary passengers emerging gratefully from badly sprung coaches to stretch their weary limbs and avail themselves of victuals and refreshment at one of the many coaching inns that lined the Market Square. Some of these public houses are still giving hospitality to travellers – though today most of them arrive by car or motorcycle.

confiscated. Crossland, forced to surrender, marched out of the castle on 22 November 1644, 'with colours flying and drums beating'.

While the Parliamentarian forces accepted this amicable surrender, they dismantled enough of the castle to ensure that it could never again be used by any side in a conflict. But they failed in their attempts to blow up the Norman castle keep, and the eastern wall still stands to its full height of 97 feet (30m), giving an idea of what an impressive fortification it had been.

The years have looked more kindly to Duncombe Park, just 1 mile (1.6km) southwest of Helmsley off the A170. Pride of place in these 600 tranquil acres (242ha) goes to the fine 200-room mansion designed by William Wakefield in 1713 as a family home for the Duncombe family and their descendants, the Fevershams. For 60 years the building was used as a girls' school, but in 1985 the present Lord and Lady Feversham took on the mammoth task of restoring the house and making it a family home once again. Now there is public access to both the house and the landscaped parkland, which boasts a terrace walk, with romantic Ionic and Tuscan temples. The temples and terrace were to have been linked by a coach drive, never completed, to the complementary Rievaulx Temple Terrace, also built by the Duncombe family.

KILBURN

The village of Kilburn has two claims to fame, both of an artistic nature – the White Horse of Kilburn and woodcarver Robert Thompson.

The White Horse, a figure cut into the turf that gazes down from Roulston Scar, and a landmark for miles around, was created by teacher John Hodgson and his pupils in 1857. It is maintained by the Kilburn White Horse Association.

Visitors to Kilburn should not miss the workshops and showrooms of Robert Thompson, a woodcarver and cabinet-maker whose fame has

KILBURN

Insight

THE 'MOUSEMAN'

Robert Thompson's signature, a carved mouse, can be found on all his pieces of furniture. But why a mouse? Thompson revealed in a letter that the idea came to him while working on a church screen. In conversation with another woodcarver he had mentioned that he was as poor as a church mouse. It seemed such an appropriate symbol that Thompson immediately adopted it for all his work.

travelled far and wide. Thompson was a self-taught craftsman whose skill remained largely unappreciated until he was commissioned to make some furniture for the local church. Encouraged by the results, Thompson began to specialise in ecclesiastical furniture. You will find that many Yorkshire churches have pews, pulpits and other fixtures made by him. One of the many pleasures of visiting them is to search for examples of the craftsman's trademark: a little carved mouse that stands proud from its surroundings. Many examples can be found in Kilburn's church, where a chapel was dedicated to the 'Mouseman' shortly before his death in 1958.

You can find Thompson's handiwork further afield – including York Minster and Westminster Abbey. Even without the mouse motif, you can recognise it by the heavy designs, the dark tones of the oak wood and the rippled effect left by the adze (a heavy hand tool with an arched cutting blade set at a right-angle to the handle). This is furniture made to last not just a lifetime, but many lifetimes.

As the business quickly expanded, Thompson's own half-timbered house became a showroom. Behind the building are more recent workshops, in which a new generation of woodworkers follows in his footsteps. Those who can't afford one of the substantial pieces of furniture can find smaller

wooden items for sale, all featuring Thompson's famous mouse. You can see stacks of neatly piled oak planks outside the workshop, being seasoned before they are used. The outbuildings house a small museum and exhibition centre.

A stream meanders through Kilburn, supplying part of its name: unusual, because here a stream is known as a beck rather than a burn. The 'burn' suffix is a clue that the origins of the village are Anglo-Saxon not Viking.

OSMOTHERLEY

This rather handsome village, on the junction of roads old and new, is the starting point of a 42-mile (67km) route march across the moors to Ravenscar, known as the Lyke Wake Walk. Every weekend hordes of walkers decant from their cars, don boots, rucksacks and cagoules, and head for the high ground. The less energetic can stroll around the village; those who manage to work up an appetite will find excellent food

Activity

A CHALLENGING WALK

The Lyke Wake Walk takes its inspiration from the old 'corpse roads', that crossed the moors, along which the deceased were carried to – often distant – burial grounds. Lyke refers to a corpse, as in a church lychgate; wake is the party after a funeral. This fine high-level walk, that lies between Osmotherley and Ravenscar, was begun in 1955 as a challenge walk – the challenge being to complete the 42 miles (67km) within 24 hours. However, the route has suffered erosion due to the pounding of too many walking boots.

on offer in the pubs that surround the old market place.

Northwest of Osmotherley is Mount Grace Priory (National Trust), though motorists need to make a rather inconvenient loop on the A19 dual carriageway to reach it. No matter – this is the best preserved of the nine Carthusian priories that were built in England. Typically,

in most European monasteries the monks lived and worked together. The Carthusian Order was particularly strict, however; the monks shunned the outside world and avoided contact with each other.

THE HAMBLETON DROVE ROAD

The Hambleton Drove Road is a vivid reminder of the days when drovers brought their cattle down from Scotland to sell at the English markets of York, Malton and beyond. This ancient ridgeway, as ruler-straight as a Roman road for much of its length, kept slow-moving cattle away from local herds and its wide verges offered free grazing on lush grass. Just as importantly, the drovers were able to avoid the tolls charged for using the turnpike roads. Many sections of the Hambleton Drove Road have been incorporated into our modern road system. The Cleveland Way uses a section of the drove road, and is easily accessed by walkers from Osmotherley.

Each monk (there were 24, including the prior) had a two-storey cell and walled garden to the back of it. Serving hatches adjacent to each cell door were ingeniously angled so that meals could be passed anonymously to the monks inside. The cells are grouped around the Great Cloister. While many of them rise no higher today than their foundations, one cell was reconstructed and furnished at the turn of the last century to show how the monks lived their solitary lives.

The Carthusian Order was founded in 1048 by St Bruno of Reims, who took Christ's sojourn in the desert as the highest example for his monks to follow. They lived like hermits avoiding worldly distractions, with most of their day given over to prayer, study and contemplation. This strict regime included a service in the middle of the night. Despite these privations, the Order grew rapidly. As late as 1530 there was a waiting list to join the Mount Grace community.

Mount Grace Priory was founded in 1398 by Thomas de Holland, with the agreement of Richard II. The monks were given land, which they rented out to tenant farmers. At the height of their wealth the income generated by the monks of Mount Grace was even greater than that of their Cistercian neighbours at Rievaulx Abbey. Yet the very success of the Carthusian communities contributed to their eventual downfall. Henry VIII ordered them to be disbanded, and in 1539 the keys to Mount Grace Priory were handed to his representatives by John Wilson, the last prior.

Visitors now enter the priory through a manor house, built in 1654 on the site of an earlier gatehouse. It houses excellent exhibitions about the priory and the daily lives of its monks. The best preserved part of the priory is the old church, whose tower still stands to its original height. Compared with other monasteries, the church is small and refreshingly simple.

OSWALDKIRK

The village of Oswaldkirk is strung out along the road beneath the steep and well-wooded Oswaldkirk Bank, and looks across Ampleforth Valley. The community takes its name from St Oswald's parish church. St Oswald became King of Northumbria at the age of 30 in AD 634, and has a special place in the history of the Christian Church. What we know about St Oswald comes largely from the *Ecclesiastical History of the English People* written by the Venerable Bede in AD 731.

Oswald was deeply impressed by the monastic community on Iona, founded by St Columba. Once a Christian convert, he grafted the new faith on to familiar customs – for example, building Christian churches on sites of pagan worship. It was Oswald who gave the island of Lindisfarne to St Aidan and the monks of Iona as another sanctuary from which to spread Christianity.

One Easter, while Oswald and Aidan were about to share a meal,

Oswald learned that there was not enough food to feed the poor at the gate. The King gave them his own food, still on its silver platter. Aidan was so moved by this act that he took the King's right hand and said 'May this hand never perish'.

Unfortunately, Oswald's faith could not save him from defeat in battle. He died in AD 642 while fighting the heathen King Penda of Mercia. Victorious Penda had Oswald's body dismembered and the pieces stuck on stakes. But, as prophesied, Oswald's right hand did not wither, and it was taken to Lindisfarne by Oswald's brother, Oswy, as a venerated relic. Thus began a cult, with Oswald being elevated to sainthood, and many tales of miraculous cures being associated with Oswald's bones.

The nave of St Oswald's church is largely Norman; cross fragments confirm that Oswaldkirk was already settled in Anglo-Saxon times. A couple of 'mother and child' sculptures in the porch offer an evocative contrast – one is modern, the other is Anglo-Saxon. Unusually, most of the rectors of Oswaldkirk are known by name; this practice started at the beginning of the 14th century and continues today.

RIEVAULX ABBEY

A short drive from Helmsley is one of Yorkshire's finest treasures. Today the setting of Rievaulx Abbey (English Heritage) is sheltered and inviting, but when Walter l' Espec dispatched a group of French monks to find a suitable site on which to build a new community it was reported to be fit only for 'wild beasts and robbers'. At that time there were no roads in the area; instead of neat copses and lush meadows there were only impenetrable thickets. To the devoutly ascetic Cistercian monks this part of the Rye Valley represented the sort of challenge on which they thrived.

In 1131, the monks began to build the mother church of the Cistercian Order in England. Many people today consider Ricvaulx to be the pre-eminent Cistercian abbey in the country. The nave is Norman, while the rest of the abbey was built in the Early English style. Enough remains of all the buildings to give visitors a very clear impression of what monastic life was like all those centuries ago.

The monks may have started out with a strictly ascetic attitude towards wealth and lifestyle; indeed the establishment of the Cistercian Order was partly due to what they considered to be the wicked corruption of the Benedictines orders. But the 140 monks and nearly 600 lay brothers of Rievaulx Abbey succeeded in creating a wealth and influence.

The monks farmed sheep, cultivated vegetables, ground corn and smelted iron, a process that required the felling of perhaps 40 trees to make a hundred-weight of metal. They even built canals to enable the iron to be transported. Stone for the buildings was brought

Insight

THE VILLAGE
Rievaulx Abbey attracted other settlers into the valley but Rievaulx village grew up only after the Reformation, and today it is a delightful little place with delectable thatched cottages of honey-coloured stone. It is rather ironic that many of the attractive houses were actually built from stone salvaged from the ruins of the abbey.

Visit

THE INVITING MOORS
About 40 per cent of the National Park is heather moorland, comprising the largest expanse in England. To see the moors at their colourful best, a sea of purple, make your visit in the late summer months when the heather is in ful bloom. The hardy, black-faced Swaledale sheep are at home on the tops, and are brought down into the valleys only at lambing times. Take care as you drive along the moorland ridge and roads, as the sheep have only the most rudimentary road sense and will dash into your path without warning.

to the site from local quarries by the same method. By 1538, when Henry VIII destroyed their way of life, the monks had become very wealthy.

Cut into the hillside above the abbey is Rievaulx Terrace (National Trust), a curved grassy promenade that is more than a match for the landscaped terrace at nearby Duncombe Park. The terrace at Rievaulx was designed in 1758. It offers strollers tantalising glimpses of the abbey between the groups of trees, with fantastic views of the Rye Valley and Hambleton Hills. There are temples, one in the Ionic style, with a fine sumptuous interior, the other Tuscan, to mark both ends of the terrace.

STOKESLEY

Now bypassed by the A172, Stokesley maintains the unhurried character of a market town. The broad verges of West Green create a little space between the Georgian façades of the houses and the main street that winds through the town.

RIEVAULX ABBEY

Stokesley still has regular markets, held every Friday on the cobbled edges of the main street. There are also busy livestock auctions and, each September, the market town is the site of one of the largest agricultural shows in the area.

The big open spaces include College Square and the market square. Behind them is Levenside, where the River Leven, little more than a stream at this point, follows its tranquil winding course between grassy banks and underneath a succession of little bridges. The oldest of these is the handsome arch of a packhorse bridge; near a ford.

With the re-drawing of the county boundaries in 1974, Stokesley slipped into Cleveland, though it has now been returned to North Yorkshire. The National Park boundary makes a detour to exclude the town and Great Ayton. While many of Stokesley's inhabitants commute to industrial Teesdale immediately to the north, Stokesley has kept its own identity.

The Cleveland Hills form a backdrop to the south as you drive northeasterly direction along the A172 between Osmotherley and Stokesley. Once used by drovers, packhorse men, pedlars and monks visiting their outlying granges, the paths of the Cleveland Hills are now used by weekend walkers.

SUTTON BANK

The view from the top of Sutton Bank is one of the finest in Yorkshire. Below you is the plain of the Vale of York. It would be hard to imagine a sharper division between the rich, arable farmland that lies to the south and the heather moors of the Hambleton Hills immediately to the north. On a clear day, armed with a pair of binoculars, you can see York Minster and the Three Peaks. Gormire Lake, directly below and almost hidden by trees, once imagined to be bottomless.

The A170 marks its midway point between the market towns of Thirsk and Helmsley by making a long 1-in-4 climb to the top of Sutton Bank. You can watch cars and lorries labouring up what is one of the steepest stretches of road in the country. For those who want to stretch their legs and enjoy the view, or for those whose engines overheat, there is a car park (and information centre) conveniently sited at the top.

From here there is a splendid, and undemanding, walk along the edge of Sutton Bank. The Yorkshire Gliding Club operates from the top of the bank, and on summer weekends the sky will be filled with slim, silent planes exploiting the thermals rising up the scar. Powered planes tow the gliders over the edge – a moment that will moisten the palms of all but the most nonchalant of flyers. With the addition of microlight aircraft, hang-gliders and, of course, soaring birds, the skies beyond Sutton Bank can get very busy indeed.

The walk continues along the top of Roulston Scar, offering views all the way, to Kilburn's White Horse – which looks best from a distance.

Thomas Taylor, a Kilburn man who made good in London, was so taken by the White Horse near Uffington that he decided to create his own. He persuaded John Hodgson, a teacher from Kilburn School, to involve his pupils in the cutting of the figure. The main problem was that his chosen hillside, while suitably steep, was not chalk-based. Hodgson commandeered his pupils to help create the outline of a horse, and used gallons of whitewash to make the design stand out.

The horse is 325 feet (99m) from head to tail, and 227 feet (69m) high. Finished in 1857, it is the only landscape figure in the north. Whitewash fades in time, so these days chalk chippings are used. A White Horse Fund has been set up for the purpose of maintaining the horse, which is a much-loved landmark. There is car park, directly beneath the White Horse, for those who don't want to walk too far. However you get to the horse, be careful not to walk on it.

TOURIST INFORMATION CENTRES
Helmsley
Helmsley Castle.
Tel: 01439 770173
Sutton Bank
Tel: 01845 597426

PLACES OF INTEREST
Byland Abbey
Coxwold.
Tel: 01347 868614
Duncombe Park
Helmsley. Tel: 01439 770213;
www.duncombepark.com
Helmsley Castle
Tel: 01439 770442
Helmsley Walled Garden
Tel: 01439 771427;
www.helmsleywalledgarden.org.uk
Mount Grace Priory
Osmotherley.
Tel: 01609 883494
Newburgh Priory
Tel: 01347 868372;
www.newburghpriory.co.uk

Rievaulx Abbey
Rievaulx.
Tel: 01439 798228
Rievaulx Terrace
Rievaulx.
Tel: 01439 798340
Shandy Hall
Coxwold.
Tel: 01347 868465

SHOPPING
MARKETS
Helmsley and Stokesley
Open-air market, Fri.

LOCAL SPECIALITIES
Furniture and Gifts
**The Mouseman Visitor Centre,
Kilburn.**
Tel: 01347 869100;
www.robertthompsons.co.uk

OUTDOOR SPORTS & ACTIVITIES

BIKE HIRE

Oswaldkirk
Golden Square Campsite,
Oswaldkirk.
Tel: 01439 788269

LONG-DISTANCE FOOTPATHS

The Cleveland Way
A 110-mile (176km) walk from
Helmsley to Filey Brigg.

The Lyke Wake Walk
A 42-mile (67km) walk from
Osmotherley to Ravenscar.

HORSE-RIDING

Boltby
Boltby Trekking Centre, Johnstone
Arms.
Tel: 01845 537392;
www.boltbytrekking.co.uk

Hawnby
Bilsdale Riding Centre,
Shaken Bridge Farm.
Tel: 01439 798252;
www.horseholiday.co.uk

ANNUAL EVENTS & CUSTOMS

Bilsdale
Bilsdale Show, Chop Gate, Aug.

Coxwold
Coxwold Fair, Jun.

Helmsley
Ryedale Festival, Jul-Aug.

Kilburn
Kilburn Feast, early to mid-Jul.

Osmotherley
Summer Games, early Jul.
Osmotherley Show, Aug.

Stokesley
Stokesley Show, Sep.

TEA ROOMS

The Angel Café Tearoom
22 High Street,
Stokesley, TS9 5QD
Tel: 01642 713622
A traditional town-centre tea room set
on the handsome main street. There's
a small area with sofas at the front of
the premises, with tables behind. All
the cakes and scones are home-made;
locals make a bee-line for the coffee
cake. The Angel also serves a range of
full meals and snacks.

The Castlegate Bakery and Café
12 Castlegate,
Helmsley, YO6 5AB
Tel: 01439 770304
Two of the specialities here are
Yorkshire Curd Tarts and traditional
Yorkshire Parkin, both made in the
bakery alongside. The traditional café
serves a generous cream tea with
its home-made scones, or try the
celebrated steak pie.

Coxwold Tearooms
School House,
Coxwold, YO61 4AD
Tel: 01347 868077
www.coxwoldschoolhouse.co.uk
You can eat in either of the two rooms,
one very cosy and the other airy, or
outside in the tea garden. You can
treat yourself to afternoon tea with
home-baking, or sample the delights of
Yorkshire ham-and-eggs.

Lord Stone's Café
Carlton Bank Car Park,
Chop Gate, TS9 7LQ
Tel: 01642 778227
This one of Britain's very few
underground cafés. Inside you'll find
that the rock-hewn room behind the
conventional café façade there's a
warm welcome and some good food,
from delicious home-made soups and
corned-beef pie to cakes and pastries.
You can also get draft beer, too – or try
the spring water; it's cool, crystal clear
and free!

BILSDALE

1662

The Black Swan Inn

Oldstead, Coxwold, YO61 4BL
Tel: 01347 868387
www.theblackswaninn.com

This is a proper country pub with a relaxed and welcoming atmosphere. As you'd expect there is real ale available in the Drovers Bar, with its flagged floor, comfy chairs and a bar made by Robert Thompson's craftsmen in nearby Kilburn. There's a pretty garden, and views of woodland and hills. The food is freshly prepared from local ingredients and also includes an impressive choice for vegetarians.

The Golden Lion

6 West End,
Osmotherley, DL6 3AA
Tel: 01609 883526

Furnished with wooden flooring and benches, this charming pub offers a wide range of ales, both local and imported. There is a superb menu, from pub food through to top-notch cuisine. The home-made burgers are delicious, and there's a good selection of fish, as well as steak and kidney pie.

The Hare Inn

Scawton, YO7 2HG
Tel: 01845 597524

This is a great place to relax, with a drink in the charming low-beamed bar (real ales, including guest beers) or a meal in the adjoining dining area. Make sure you leave room for a pudding – you'll find the lemon possett, among others, is excellent.

The Wombwell Arms

Wass, YO61 4BE
Tel: 01347 868280

There are two bistro-style restaurants, serving a menu that includes steak and Guinness pie, as well as plenty of local produce and fish. The bars stock a good range of Yorkshire ales, including Black Sheep and Timothy Taylor's.

Central Moors

CROPTON FOREST

FARNDALE

HOVINGHAM

HUTTON-LE-HOLE

KIRKBYMOORSIDE

LASTINGHAM

NUNNINGTON

ROSEDALE

STANDING STONES

WHEELDALE

INTRODUCTION

The central moors include high moorland, beautiful valleys and some delectable villages. The North Yorkshire Moors Railway runs through the wooded Newtondale Gorge on the edge of Cropton Forest, which offers a host of leisure possibilities, from energetic cycling and riding through to easy strolls and quiet picnics. To the north of the forest is Roman Road on Wheeldale, a well-preserved section of road thought to be of Roman origin.

HOT SPOTS

Unmissable attractions

Discover the remains of a Roman road on Wheeldale Moor...visit Nunnington Hall to see the miniature rooms...walk across the moors to Lilla Cross, the oldest on the North York Moors...climb the one-in-two hill called Rosedale Chimney out of Rosedale Abbey...sit quietly in the crypt at Lastingham church for an experience of early history...hire a bike and follow the track of the former Rosedale Railway...have lunch at the Spa Tea rooms of Hovingham Bakery...visit Farndale in spring for the superb display of wild daffodils...take the road across the moors from Rosedale Abbey to Egton Bridge when the heather is blooming...have dinner in the garden at the famed Star Inn at Harome...travel through Newtondale Gorge on the North Yorkshire Moors Railway.

1 Nunnington Hall
The lovely old manor house of Nunnington Hall dates mainly from the 17th century. It is set in beautiful gardens on the banks of the River Rye.

2 Chimney Bank
Wonderful scenery unfolds from the top of snow-capped Chimney Bank, between the villages of Rosedale Abbey and Hutton-le-Hole.

3 Cyclists at snow-covered Rosedale
Cycling the quiet back roads over the central moors is a popular way to explore the National Park, whatever the season.

4 Rosedale Abbey Sundial
As the name of the village suggests, Rosedale Abbey was once the site of a small Cistercian priory founded in 1158. Little remains of the original building (the stone was reclaimed for building houses in the village and the new church) except a turret staircase and a sundial.

5 Ryedale Folk Museum
An amazing collection of rural buildings rescued from all around the North York Moors have been reconstructed in a hamlet setting behind the modest entrance to this museum of local life.

Ryedale
Folk
Museum

5

CROPTON FOREST

The moors are continually evolving, and one of the most dramatic changes of the 20th century was the creation of large-scale conifer plantations. The Forestry Commission began the process in the 1920s; now the area comprises one of the most extensive man-made forests inthe country. Cropton Forest occupies a large area of the North Riding Forest Park between Rosedale in the west and Newtondale to the east. Conifer planting on this scale has not met with universal approval; many feel that well-loved views have been unfairly smothered beneath the starkly dark geometric shapes of these plantations. Nevertheless, the afforestation of what had mostly been moorland and poor-quality farmland brought much-needed employment to many rural areas.

The woodlands are now reaching maturity, and upwards of 120,000 tonnes of timber are felled every year to meet consumer demand for softwoods. More recently, greater care has been taken to ensure that plantings harmonise with their surroundings. Areas of broadleaved and mixed woods provide a more varied habitat for wildlife, and are easier on the eye than vast, uniform conifer plantations.

Cropton Forest provides plenty of outdoor activities – there is a campsite, forest cabins and educational outdoor activity centres set out amid the trees, and plenty of opportunities for walking and biking. The North Yorkshire Moors Railway, from Pickering to Grosmont, passes through the eastern edge of the forest, and stations at Levisham and Newtondale provide easy access for visitors to the woodland.

Roman roads are not hard to find, on the map at least. The Roman road, commonly known as Wade's Causeway, across Wheeldale Moor, is immediately to the north of Cropton Forest, is still that rare thing – a Roman road which is still visible on the ground.

Activity

BACK TO NATURE

The recreational possibilities of Cropton Forest are now being realised. On any summer weekend you will see mountain bikers tackling the forest trails, walkers following well-waymarked footpaths and families enjoying themselves at the many picnic sites and adventure playgrounds. Those who prefer their nature 'red in tooth and claw' will head for the solitude of the breezy moor-tops. The Newtondale Horse Trail, offers 35 miles (56km) of bracing, traffic-free riding. Local riding stables hire out horses by the hour or day.

There are fascinating Roman remains to be seen at Cawthorn Camp, which is believed to have been as a training camp, signposted from the minor road between the villages of Cropton and Newton-on-Rawcliffe. From the purpose-built car park the waymarked path, no more than a mile (1.6km) long, guides you around them. The well-preserved earthworks reveal a camp, two forts and an annexe wedged side by side on a plateau, which enjoys panoramic views to the north across Cropton Forest to the moors beyond. By the year AD 122, when the Emperor Hadrian was constructing his famous wall to the north, the Cawthorn camps had been abandoned.

FARNDALE

Farndale is a delightful valley at any time of the year, but every Eastertime it blooms with a profusion of golden wild daffodils. The daffodil walk accompanies the River Dove between Low Mill and Church Houses. This is an undeniably pleasant stroll, and suitable for wheelchairs, but try to pick a weekday, if possible, to make your visit; or venture a little further afield, for wild daffodils can be found throughout the valley. The traffic has become so heavy in recent years that a field in the village of Low Mill becomes a car park while

FARNDALE

the daffodils are in bloom. There is a useful park-and-ride bus service operating from Kirkbymoorside and Hutton-le-Hole.

But why Farndale? And why in such profusion? Farndale's blooms are wild, short-stemmed daffodils; stories variously attribute their planting to the monks of Rievaulx, and to Father Postgate, a Catholic priest who was persecuted for his faith. We merely know that wild daffodils have flourished in these dales for centuries.

The greatest threat to the daffodils has been the ever-increasing numbers of visitors, who were once unable to admire the spectacular springtime displays without gathering armfuls of the flowers. Once market traders found this free source of daffodils the flowers were in danger, and in 1953 about 2,000 acres (810ha) of Farndale were designated as a nature reserve; the daffodils are safe for us all to enjoy. Resist the temptation to pick any.

At other times of the year Farndale reverts to being a peaceful farming community. Both sides of the valley are accessible; from either Kirkbymoorside and Hutton-le-Hole on the A170 to the south, or, most dramatically, from the north down a steep road which descends from Blakey Ridge just to the south of the Lion Inn.

Insight

MAULEY CROSS

Moorland crosses are generally fairly reliable indicators that an old thoroughfare, or crossroads, is near at hand. Mauley Cross stands on the route of one of the oldest known roads across the moors to have survived, which may date from Roman times. The cross stands where the track meets the medieval Brown Howe Road. It is named after the de Mauley family of Mulgrave Castle near Whitby and probably marked the limits of grazing rights. The cross once stood on open moorland.

HOVINGHAM

One of North Yorkshire's prettiest villages, Hovingham, lies on the route of an old Roman road from Malton to Boroughbridge. When the foundations of Hovingham Hall were being laid, in 1745, Roman remains were unearthed, including part of a bath house. The Hall's first owner, Sir Thomas Worseley, was a descendant of Oliver Cromwell. His passion for horses led him to build the stable block facing on to the village green. In a rather unusual arrangement, visitors have to pass through the stable block to reach the Hall's main entrance. The Hall is mainly open to private parties by prior arrangement.

The attractive architectural unity of the surrounding houses, the neat layout with broad grass verges and an air of gentility all mark Hovingham out as an estate village. One of the Hall's lawns is today the village's cricket pitch; surely one of the loveliest grounds on which to watch or play the summer game.

Insight

SARKLESS KITTY

The dales are rich in folklore; one story tells of Kitty Garthwaite, 'Sarkless Kitty', from the village of Lowna Bridge, who, more than 200 years ago, was 'walking out' with Willie Dixon of Hutton-le-Hole. A rumour came to Kitty that Willie was seeing another lass. A lovers' tiff by the River Dove was followed, tragically, by Kitty's being found drowned in a pool, wearing only her 'sark', or petticoat. After their argument, Willie had ridden to York to get a marriage licence. On his return his horse stumbled and Willie drowned in the same pool where Kitty had earlier been found. The ghost of Kitty, naked but carrying her sark over her arm, is said to haunt the riverside spot where the lovers had kept their trysts.

The houses at the northern end of the village are clustered either side of a pretty little beck, with a ford, where ducks swim and await visitors who may have bread for them.

HUTTON-LE-HOLE

It is to Hutton-le-Hole's benefit that it lies just off the main A170 between Thirsk and Scarborough, for it, unlike its larger neighbours, has managed to maintain its distinct personality instead of selling its soul to the albeit profitable tourist trade. One of Yorkshire's 'picture postcard' villages, its houses are set back from Hutton Beck, a little watercourse spanned by a succession of pretty little bridges. The village green is the size of a meadow, but the grass is cropped short by grazing sheep, which wander wherever they choose – as likely as not in the middle of the road, so take care to avoid them.

The houses of discreet grey stone, with the red-tiled roofs so typical of the moors, lend a timeless air to the village. The tiny church has some very fine oak furniture made by Robert Thompson of Kilburn; a close examination will reveal the trademark carved mouse that can be found on his work.

Insight

RYEDALE'S WITCH POST

The cruck-framed house at the Ryedale Folk Museum contains one of the rarest examples of a witch post to have survived – most of which are found in the north of England. This post, of mountain ash, is elaborately carved with a cross and other, more ambiguous, symbols. It stands by the fireplace, so it would be passed by anyone who came into the living area, and also had the practical purpose of supporting the beam across the inglenook. It was designed, of course, to ward off evil spirits and protect those who sat here enjoying the fire's warmth.

Once you have seen the village, don't neglect to visit Ryedale Folk Museum. This open-air collection is based on the displays of bygones built up by two local collectors. From its beginnings in a single old farm building, the museum has expanded far beyond its walls, to include many other vernacular buildings – brought

171

Insight

CRUCK-FRAMED HOUSES

The crucks and their cross-beams made a shape like the letter 'A'; these heavy timbers supported the entire weight of the building's roof, allowing the walls to be infilled. Since the walls were not load bearing, it was an easy matter to alter the position of doors, or create windows.

stone by stone to the museum and painstakingly re-erected.

For nearly 500 years a thatched, cruck-framed cottage has stood here in Danby village. In 1967 this typical farmer's house was moved to the museum's impressive 2.5-acre (1ha) site. The tall, 16th-century manor house, also thatched and cruck-framed, is a huge hall open to the roof beams. This was once the meeting place of the Manor Court, where disputes were settled and common rights safeguarded. Other museum buildings house a primitive 16th-century glass furnace,

a photographer's studio, and a row of shops recreated as they would have looked more than a hundred years ago.

Throughout these buildings, exhibits in their own right, are informal displays showing what life was like in such moorland villages in bygone days. The site is also the venue for various events which are held through the year.

KIRKBYMOORSIDE

The market town of Kirkbymoorside lies on the edge of the moors just outside the National Park, on the A170 between Helmsley and Pickering. Don't judge the place by first appearances; you should leave the main road to investigate the old heart of the town. The broad main street is lined with inns, a reminder that Kirkbymoorside was an important halt in the days of stage coaches. The oldest inn is the Black Swan, whose elaborately carved entrance porch bears the date 1632. The market cross, mounted on a

Road
to:Pic
krino
r:Mal
ton:

Insight

ST GREGORY'S SUNDIAL

The engraved inscription on the Saxon sundial, which is embedded into the wall of the church of St Gregory's Minster is in Old English. Translated it reads 'Orm, the son of Gamal, bought St Gregory's Church when it was utterly broken down and fallen, and he rebuilt it from ground level, to Christ and St Gregory, in the days of King Edward and Earl Tostig. Howarth made me and Brand the priest. This is sun's marker at all times'. The Edward of the inscription is King Edward the Confessor, who ruled between 1042 and 1066; Tostig became Earl of Northumberland in 1055; Howarth made the sundial; Brand was the name of the parish priest. This brief inscription is the longest example of Anglo-Saxon carving to have survived.

stepped base, can be found in a side street near by. Market day is Wednesday, as it has been since medieval times.

Kirkbymoorside has a road called Castlegate. Once it had a castle too, on a hill behind the parish church, but stones salvaged from its ruins were used to build the 17th-century tollbooth in the market place. Another fortified building was once a hunting lodge built by the Neville family. The church, though old, was largely rebuilt last century.

Lovers of beautiful old churches should rejoin the A170 and travel westwards in the direction of Helmsley for just a few hundred yards, before following the sign for St Gregory's Minster. If the word 'minster' conjures up some grand edifice, you will be surprised to find a tiny, dignified church built of grey stone, almost hidden away in beautiful, secluded Kirkdale.

This ancient building was dedicated to St Gregory – the pope who dispatched St Augustine to preach Christianity to the pagan English in AD 597. There has long been a church here, certainly before Anglo-Saxon times, as it had to be rebuilt in c1060, perhaps as a result of Viking destruction.

Recent excavations have revealed a prehistoric standing stone by the west tower, possible evidence of Christians reusing a pagan site. Many visitors ask: why a minster? And why here, in such an isolated spot? The term 'minster' is derived from the Latin *monasterium*, which denoted a community of priests or monks who used the church as a base from which to serve the surrounding countryside before the parish church system evolved. This status has remained with churches; some like this one are relatively small, some like York Minster are large and important.

We can be more certain about the dates of the rebuilding because ancient – yet tantalisingly brief – details are carved on a sundial mounted over the south door. The sun doesn't reach it any more; to protect the sundial, the best Anglo-Saxon example known, a porch was added in the 19th century.

LASTINGHAM

The casual visitor to the small village of Lastingham will see a collection of good-looking houses, a few wellheads and a welcoming inn, but Lastingham has something more to offer – a unique place in the history of Christianity.

St Cedd left the island of Lindisfarne (Holy Island) in AD 655 and chose this site on which to build a monastery. It was an area which, according to the Venerable Bede, was 'the lurking place of robbers and wild beasts'. St Cedd was buried in his monastery, close to the altar. This early building was later sacked by invading Danes.

In 1078 Abbot Stephen of Whitby moved his own community to Lastingham. He built a crypt dedicated to St Cedd, in which the saint's remains were re-interred. Apart from cosmetic changes (and the stairs leading down into it from the nave of the church above) the crypt looks the way it did almost a thousand years ago.

Itself a church in miniature, the crypt has a chancel, aisles, Norman pillars, a low vaulted roof and a stone slab for an altar. Here, too, are fragments of ancient crosses. It was to have been part of a large abbey, but Abbot Stephen's plans were thwarted and the community moved to the site of St Mary's Abbey, York.

The present church, planned merely as the abbey's chancel, was eventually consolidated to meet local congregational needs. Today, visitors come from further afield to see a building that has happily survived years of neglect and clumsy 'restorations'. A closer examination of two of the village's wellheads reveal that one is dedicated to St Cedd, the other to his more famous brother, St Chad, who succeeded him as Abbot of Lastingham.

If you're a real ale enthusiast, Cropton Brewery, 1.5 miles (2.5km) east of Lastingham, is the place to head. It brews up to 60 barrels a week. Open daily during season, and by arrangement in the winter.

NUNNINGTON

At Nunnington a delightful 17th-century three-arched bridge spans the River Rye. From one of its embrasures (the V-shaped spaces constructed to shield pedestrians from the traffic) you can gaze down into the water and try to spot basking trout, superbly camouflaged against the sandy river bed. Set in beautiful gardens across the river is honey-coloured Nunnington Hall. This tranquil setting offers no clue to the hall's turbulent past.

Nunnington Hall's early history is sketchy; it is thought to have been built on the site of a nunnery – hence its name. It passed through many hands, including the Abbot of St Mary's, York. Another later owner, Viscount Preston, served James II as Secretary of State for Scotland; charged later with treason, he escaped the gallows only by implicating his fellow conspirators.

While the hall's west wing can be dated to 1580, most of the building, a concoction of Tudor and

Stuart styles, was built during the 17th century. The Hall, housing the entrancing Carlisle collection of miniature rooms and a display by the British Toymakers Guild, is now cared for by the National Trust.

Nunnington's handsome houses in grey stone are hidden from sight to those who drive straight through the village; it's better to explore on foot. Nunnington's church, with its double dedication to St James and All Saints, dates largely from the 13th century. Here, in an alcove, is the effigy of a knight in chain mail. This recumbent figure commemorates Sir Walter de Teyes, Lord of the Manor of Nunnington and Stonegrave until his death in 1325.

ROSEDALE

Rosedale is a lovely tranquil valley today, echoing with the bubbling cry of the curlew and the distant barking of farm dogs. City visitors will feel themselves to be a long way from the noise and grime of Yorkshire's industrial heartlands. But appearances can be deceptive. Just 100 years ago the scene was very different: Rosedale was a veritable moorland 'Klondike'.

Ironstone had been mined here, sporadically, since the Iron Age. During the 13th century mining added to the wealth of the monks of Byland Abbey; but it was only in the middle of the 19th century that the extent of Rosedale's subterranean wealth was realised, with the discovery of massive quantities of top-grade iron ore. The Industrial Revolution brought a huge demand for iron; the blast furnaces on the Rivers Tees and Tyne needed a constant supply for building ships, railways and general engineering. Other mines were driven – at Glaisdale, Beck Hole and on the coast, for example – but the mines at Rosedale proved to be the most productive in the area.

The transport of ore was difficult from isolated Rosedale. In 1861 the North Eastern Railway Company built a line from Battersby Junction

Insight

YORKSHIRE'S 'KLONDIKE'

Between 1850–70 the population of Rosedale quadrupled, as the iron mines were driven deep into the valley sides. A system of underground passages was dug, consolidated by wooden supports. The miners excavated to either side of these tunnels, with pick and shovel, to win the ore-bearing rock. The news soon spread, with experienced miners converging on Rosedale from all over the country – and particularly from Cornwall and Wales. At the height of production, more than 5,000 men found work here.

on the Stockton–Whitby line, over the bleak moorland to Rosedale West. In 1865 a branch was built around the head of Rosedale to the east mines, joining the original line at Blakey Junction, just below the Lion Inn on Blakey Ridge. To reach Teesside the wagons, now laden with ore, were winched down the steep descent of the Ingleby Incline. The engines that plied the high-level line between the Rosedale mines and the incline never came down from their moorland heights, except when they had to be repaired.

The Rosedale railway was closed in 1929, by which time the valley's mining boom was over. Though the demand for iron was as buoyant as ever, ore could be mined more cheaply elsewhere. The route of this fascinating line is used today by walkers, cyclists and horse riders. The valley is quietly 'going back to nature', but the massive calcining kilns (where ironstone was roasted to reduce its weight) are being preserved, so that Rosedale's mining past will not be forgotten.

You will search in vain for the abbey that gave the village of Rosedale Abbey its name. The ladies who serve in the tea shops answer the question with a weary resignation that suggests this is not the first time they've been asked. The truth is that you can see the remains of the abbey (it was actually

Activity

CYCLING IN ROSEDALE

The old Rosedale railway is ideal for cycling for much of its length, as it is relatively level and surfaced with ash ballast. The best section is from Rosedale Bank Top to Blakey Junction, near the Lion Inn (4 miles/6.8km) and then across the moors to Ingleby Bank Top, another 7 miles (11.9km). You could even cycle down the incline – but remember what goes down must come up again.

a priory) wherever you look: the population explosion of the mid-19th century meant that the priory was plundered for its building stone to build homes for the ironstone miners. Whether this is seen as the desecration of a religious site, or the sensible recycling of a valuable resource, depends on your own reading of history. The priory was founded in 1158 as a Cistercian nunnery by William of Rosedale. It was never a large establishment:

there were probably only nine nuns and a prioress living here.

St Lawrence's Church stands on the site of the priory's chapel. To find a couple of relics from the earlier building, walk up to the altar rail. One of the stones set into the floor here bears a carved cross and, faintly, the name Maria, in memory of one of the nuns. Beyond the altar rail is an ancient stone seat from the nunnery; it is carved from a single block of stone.

STANDING STONES

It is appropriate that Ralph Cross should have been chosen as the emblem of the National Park, for standing stones and wayside crosses are one of the most its most intriguing features. No other area can boast so many examples.

Within the National Park boundary there are more than a thousand stones raised by man, standing witness to many centuries of settlement on the moors. The moorland stones are known as

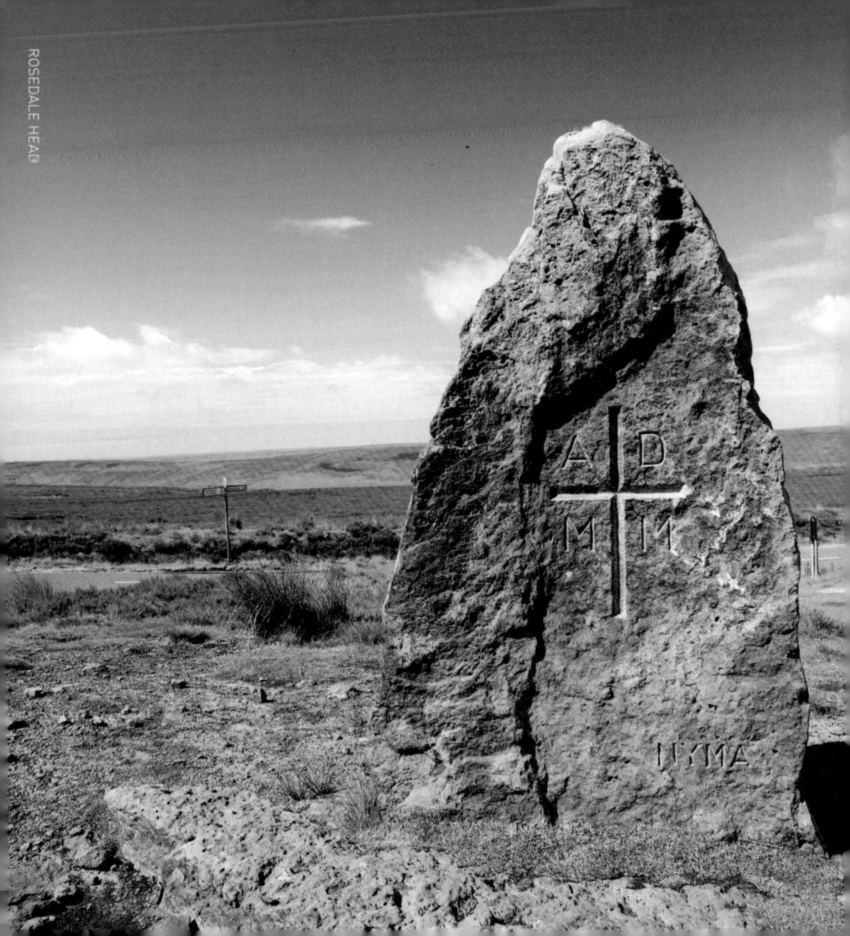

ROSEDALE HEAD

ROSEDALE MILLENNIUM CROSS

'crosses', even though only a small proportion of them are actually carved into the shape of a cross. Some are simple monoliths fitted with side-pieces to make a cruciform shape. One particular design, repeated in many moorland crosses, is known as the wheelhead. It consisted of a widening of the top of a stone, which is pierced with four holes to create the shape of a cross. Other stones simply have the design of a cross carved into their surface.

The moorland crosses weren't erected at random; they were put up for a variety of reasons. A number of them were preaching crosses, marking the spot where itinerant monks would attempt to bring the gospel to the pagan Anglo-Saxon communities. If the monks were successful and their words fell on willing ears, a church might be built on, or near, the site of the cross.

In the Middle Ages other crosses were put up as waymarkers, to guide travellers across the largely featureless expanses of

Visit

EARLY SIGNPOSTS

Stone signposts were erected at all the crossroads on the moors in 1711 by order of the Justices at Northallerton, to prevent travellers from getting hopelessly lost. They sign the direction of each road to the nearest main town, and sometimes the distances. The spelling is distinctly idiosyncratic, and some have primitive hands carved on them. There is a good example about 2 miles (3.2km) north out of Hutton-le-Hole on the road to Ralph Cross.

'Blackamore'. Moorland roads were established by frequent usage; they weren't 'built' like the Roman roads; at best, the routes might be delineated by a line of causeway stones. The moorland crosses would help to mark the route, and offer weary travellers further targets in the distance to aim for. Other crosses were erected to mark the boundaries of the monastic sheep-grazing land.

Activity

THE CROSSES WALK

The Crosses Walk is a challenge walk of about 53 miles (84.8km), created to be undertaken in a single day. Starting and finishing at the village of Goathland, it uses thirteen prominent crosses for their original purpose, as waymarkers.

During these times the building of bridges and wayside crosses was seen as an act of piety. Many rich men would attempt to improve their heavenly chances by such good works. So, here too, a stone shaped as a cross would reflect both the donor's good intentions and the travellers' gratitude to find another waymark. It's hard for us to imagine how reassuring it would have been to see a moorland cross appear in the mist. The spiritual aspect of these moorland crosses was emphasised by the custom of leaving coins on them – many had an indentation on the top for needy travellers.

Many stone crosses on the moorland now exist only as empty 'sockets' or just names on old maps. However, at least 30 of the moorland crosses still stand to their full height. Ralph Cross, at 9 feet (2.75m) high on the top of Blakey Ridge, is also known as Young Ralph. It has been a familiar landmark for centuries, since it marks a meeting of important tracks. Now it can be seen by motorists driving between Castleton and Hutton-le-Hole. Close by are two more crosses: 'Old Ralph' is 4 feet (1.2m) high, while 'Fat Betty' comprises a rounded stone 'head' on a square stone 'body'.

The oldest cross still standing on the moors is reckoned to be Lilla Cross, off the Whitby–Pickering road at Ellerbeck Bridge. Possibly of 10th-century origin, it is said to mark the final resting place of Lilla, a minister to King Edwin, whose kingdom encompassed the Yorkshire Wolds. Lilla saved the life of his king by falling on to the sword of an assassin, but inevitably died in the process. King Edwin commemorated this selfless act with the cross you can still see today.

WHEELDALE

The Romans made few incursions into what we now know as the North York Moors. The inescapable conclusion is that the wastes of what for centuries was known as 'Blackamore' held few attractions for the colonists. However, they may have built a road across the moors to link a settlement at Malton with the signal stations on the coast near Goldsborough and Whitby.

A section of road on Wheeldale Moor, just over a mile (1.6km) in length and known as Wade's Causeway, is reckoned to be the best-preserved Roman road in the country, though doubts have been expressed in recent years about its Roman origins. The road gradually fell into disuse, eventually disappearing beneath the encroaching heather and bracken. It was rediscovered in 1914.

It can be reached by driving north from Pickering on an unclassified road. Once past the village of Stape, follow the Wheeldale Road with Cropton Forest on the right and the expanse of Wheeldale Moor to the left. Park your car near to the watersplash at Wheeldale Bridge, and the old Roman road is immediately ahead. The Roman Road over Wheeldale is also signposted from the village of Goathland, west of the A169.

The Romans' innovative road-making skills are legendary, yet this particular road looks a rather rocky thoroughfare. That's because what you can see is the road's foundations, made up of large stones set into gravel. The original road surface would have been smoother, overlaid with finer aggregate. The road is cambered so that water would drain off and be carried away in culverts. You can follow the route and decide for yourself whether or not you are walking in the footsteps of Roman legions.

CENTRAL MOORS

TOURIST INFORMATION CENTRE
Hutton-le-Hole
Ryedale Folk Museum.
Tel: 01751 417367

PLACES OF INTEREST
Cawthorne
Remains of Roman camp on road
between Cropton and Newton-on-
Rawcliffe.
Nunnington Hall
Nunnington.
Tel: 01439 748283
Ryedale Folk Museum
Hutton-le-Hole.
Tel: 01751 417367;
www.ryedalefolkmuseum.co.uk

SHOPPING
MARKETS
Kirkbymoorside
Open-air market, Wed.

LOCAL SPECIALITIES
Ceramics
James Brooke, The Pottery,
Appleton-le-Moors.
Tel: 01751 417514
Glass
Gillies Jones Glass Design, The Old
Forge,
Rosedale Abbey.
Tel: 01751 417550;
www.gilliesjonesglass.co.uk

SPORTS & ACTIVITIES
HORSE-RIDING
Newtondale Horse Trail
35 traffic-free miles (56km). Guidebook
from North York Moors National Park
Authority
Sinnington
Friars Hill Riding Stables.
Tel: 01751 432758;
www.friarshillstables.co.uk

MOUNTAIN BIKING & CYCLE HIRE
Cropton
Donald Wilkie Bike Hire, Keldy Forest
Cabins, Cropton Forest.
Tel: 01751 417510 (summer only).
North York Moors Mountain Bike
Routes; www.muddybums.org.uk

WATERSPORTS
Sutherland Lodge Activity Centre,
Cropton.
Tel: 01751 417228
Canoeing.

ANNUAL EVENTS & CUSTOMS
Hutton-le-Hole
World Merrills Championships (board
game), Sep.
Farndale
Farndale Show, Aug.
Rosedale
Rosedale Show, Aug.
Ryedale
Ryedale Show, Kirkbymoorside, Jul.

TEA ROOMS

Hovingham Bakery Spa Tearoom
Brookside, Hovingham, YO62 4LG
Tel: 01653 628898
The Bakery provides delicious fresh
bread and cakes to locals and visitors,
and serves them in its little tea room
by the beck – you can sit outside on
summer days. The hearty sandwiches
are a meal in themselves, and there
are excellent cream teas – the fruit
scones are a particular favourite.

Nunnington Hall
Nunnington, YO62 5UY
Tel: 01439 748283
www.nationaltrust.org.uk
As you'd expect from the National
Trust, the food is top-notch. Cream
teas, cakes (try the special Nunnington
Fruit Loaf) and light lunches will tempt
you. If you're there later in the season,
you'll find old apple varieties from the
orchard used in pies, flans, crumbles,
soups and chutneys – worth making a
special autumn journey for!

Abbey Tea Rooms and Store
Rosedale Abbey, YO18 9SA
Tel: 01751 417475
As well as plain, fruit and cheese
scones, you can find cherry scones,
scones made with treacle, scones
made with blueberries and ginger...
and you can spread them with
blueberry and lavender jam. If you're
more peckish, try the Yorkshire Ham
afternoon tea.

Lastingham Grange
Lastingham, YO62 6TH
Tel: 01751 417345
www.lastinghamgrange.com
Take tea in this elegant hotel on the
hillside on the edge of Lastingham. The
traditional afternoon teas are served in
the drawing room, where you can loll
on comfy chintz sofas in front of the fire
– it's almost like visiting the gracious
home of a wealthy great-aunt.

CHURCH HOUSES

ROSEDALE

The Lion Inn

Blakey Ridge, Kirkbymoorside,
YO62 7LQ
Tel: 01751 417320
www.lionblakey.co.uk

The Lion is set on the high moors at the heart of the National Park. Expect to rub shoulders with walkers and mountain-bikers, as well as lovers of real ale and those who enjoy well-cooked, substantial meals, eaten either in the restaurant or the bar. You're sure of a warm welcome, whatever the weather at this exposed spot.

The New Inn

Cropton, Nr Pickering, YO18 8HH
Tel: 01751 417330
www.croptonbrewery.com

The Cropton micro-brewery produces some fine ales that you can sample in its own pub, the New Inn. There is good food available, too, using local ingredients, including fish from Whitby. You can eat either in the cosy bar or in the elegant restaurant.

The Star Inn

Harome, Nr Helmsley, YO62 5JE.
Tel: 01439 770397
www.thestaratharome.co.uk

While you're welcome to drop in for a drink (hand-pulled beers, a good selection of wines) it's the Michelin-rated food that is the draw. It is superb, though not cheap. There's a shop selling home-made delicacies.

The George and Dragon

Market Place, Kirkbymoorside,
YO62 6AA
Tel: 01751 433334
www.georgeanddragon.net

The George caters for visitors and locals, who enjoy its historic atmosphere. There's real ale on tap and more than 50 types of whisky. The good food is available either in the restaurant or bistro, or by the fire in the bar. The menu is strong on fresh seafood and fish.

Eastern Moors & Coast

INTRODUCTION

The eastern moors is the triangle formed between Whitby, Scarborough and Pickering. The coastline provides spectacular cliffs, hidden coves, sandy beaches and fascinating rock formations. To preserve the area's unique character, many miles have been designated Heritage Coast. Robin Hood's Bay is one of the loveliest fishing villages in the country, whilst Scarborough has been Yorkshire's premier seaside resort since Victorian times.

HOT SPOTS

Unmissable attractions

Explore Levisham and Lockton, a pair of delectable moorland villages
and discover one of the earliest sites for Iron Age smelting on the nearby
moors...explore the beautiful Forge Valley, which is a haven for wildlife...
negotiate the Hole of Horcum, sometimes known as the Devil's Punchbowl,
a huge natural amphitheatre scooped out of Levisham Moor...ride high on
the restored North Yorkshire Moors Railway, steam-hauled trains taking you
deep into the moors...explore the charming resort of Robin Hood's Bay...
treat yourself to a day out at Scarborough, one of Britain's oldest medicinal
spas and a traditional bucket-and-spade seaside resort.

1

1 **Hole of Horcum**
Otherwise known as the Devil's Punchbowl, this deep-sided, natural hollow offers plenty of good opportunities for walks.

2 **Robin Hood's Bay**
With its cobbled streets and tiny cottages, Robin Hood's Bay is one of the loveliest fishing villages in the north of England.

203

3

4 Quoits in Goathland
The game of quoits is played in many moorland villages. The object is to throw a heavy iron quoit over the peg, a metal pin, but there's much more to it than that, as you'll discover if you watch seasoned players, like these in Goathland.

5 Scarborough rock pools
These young holiday-makers are well equipped to explore the fascinating rock pools exposed at low tide in Scarborough.

3 North Yorkshire Moors Railway
During the summer months steam trains haul their passengers through some of the finest scenery of the North York Moors.

4

5

BROMPTON

Motorists on the A170 tend to drive straight through Brompton in their haste to get to the superb sands of the Yorkshire coast. In doing so they miss a gem. The pretty little village is set around a small lake, into which the church doors were thrown during the Civil War; they were later recovered and re-hung. The poet William Wordsworth took the time to get to know the village, for he courted Mary Hutchinson, a local girl who lived at Gallows Hill Farm. When they married, in 1802, it was in Brompton's 14th-century church. The wedding ceremony was recorded in her diary by his sister Dorothy; she even joined the happy couple on their honeymoon in Grasmere, in the Lake District.

The village has a unique (though sadly little-known) place in the history of aeronautics. Everybody knows it was Wilbur and Orville Wright who made the first manned flight, in their flimsy craft, Kittyhawk. Yet a remarkable 50 years before that memorable occasion, an unsung squire of Brompton Hall quietly set about building a flying machine.

Brompton Hall (now a school and not open to the public) had been the home of the Cayley family since Stuart times, and Sir George Cayley (1771–1857) developed an unquenchable scientific curiosity. This was an age when enthusiastic amateurs, especially those blessed

Insight

A RELUCTANT VOLUNTEER

Taking to heart the notion 'Why have a dog and bark yourself?', Sir George Cayley volunteered his understandably reluctant coachman to make the first manned flight. On a still day in 1853 the glider made a short 55-yard (50m) hop across Brompton Dale. The coachman, relieved to have survived unscathed, but unwilling to entertain thoughts of another death-defying flight, resigned on the spot, telling Sir George that he was paid to drive, not to fly.

BRACKEN

with private incomes, could indulge their whims in the arts and sciences. Sir George, however, was no mere dabbler; his inventions included caterpillar tracks and a new form of artificial limb, prompted by an accident to one of his estate workers. Seeing how the River Derwent regularly flooded the flat countryside, to the chagrin of local farmers, he designed and constructed a sea cut to divert flood waters straight into the North Sea near Scarborough.

But the prospect of flight remained Sir George's passion. Even before the 18th century was out he was designing gliders – continuing to refine the craft's aerodynamics until he had a controllable machine that could carry a man. He had already experimented with propellers, abandoning them merely because the internal combustion engine was not even on the horizon. His various experiments proved that a contoured wing could provide much greater lift than a wing with a flat profile.

Visit

THE COLOURFUL MOORS

Leave Goathland in any direction and you will soon find yourself on expansive heather moorland. Though blackened in winter (hence the old name for the moors: 'Blackamore') the heather bursts into life during July, August and September, when miles of tiny flowers paint the uplands in glorious purple. The bell heather has deep purple flowers, while those of the cross-leaved heather have a pinker hue. The scene is made even more colourful during late summer by the blue-black bilberries and the rich brown bracken.

Though an inscription in the church porch acknowledges Sir George as the 'Father of Aeronautics', his pioneering efforts are largely overlooked. Facing the main road through the village is the six-sided building, the summerhouse, now boarded up, unfortunately, where Sir George worked on his flying machines.

EASTERN MOORS & COAST

COATHLAND

This pleasant village has achieved
fame by proxy as the location
for the popular television series
Heartbeat. On the small screen
Goathland is transformed into
fictional Aidensfield, where PC Rob
Walker (actor Jonathan Kerrigan)
treads his rural beat. Episodes
were filmed throughout the moors,
but the village of Goathland will be
especially familiar to viewers; there
is no need to search for locations the
cameras have blessed.

Goathland was a popular
destination for visitors long before
the television series began, and
though by no means the prettiest
village on the moors, it is certainly
well worth visiting in its own right.
The broad grass verges, closely
cropped by sheep, lead directly on
to the heather and bracken of the
moors. The village also makes an
excellent centre for exploring the
surrounding moorland and the
stretch of Roman road known as
Wade's Causeway. Fame brings

its own problems, however, and
Goathland does get very busy on
Bank Holidays.

Black-faced moorland sheep
are everywhere, local farmers enjoy
grazing rights throughout the village,
so the sheep roam where they will
with a distinctly proprietorial air.
They are so tame and accustomed to
visitors that they will come right up
to cars and picnickers in search of
tasty morsels. Resist the temptation
to offer them food. They keep the
grass closely cropped, but have only
the most rudimentary road sense, so
care is required as you drive through
the village.

A brief investigation of the
village and its surroundings will
reveal a number of delightful
waterfalls. The best known is the
70-foot (21m) Mallyan Spout, easily
reached via a footpath adjacent to
the Mallyan Spout Hotel. The hotel's
Victorian architecture is a reminder
that the first influx of visitors came
with the building of the railway in
the 1830s. Before that, the village's

moorland setting kept it in relative isolation. Goathland's church, just a century old, but on a site of Christian worship for a thousand years, was furnished by Robert Thompson of Kilburn. Look for the little carved mice that were the craftsman's trademark. Near the church is a pinfold, a small, square paddock enclosed by stone walls, where stray beasts could be corralled until claimed by their owners.

Goathland was one of the stations on the main Whitby–Pickering line, a status it retains now that the once-defunct line has a new lease of life as the North Yorkshire Moors Railway. The steepest section of the line was known as the Beck Hole Incline, and it was so steep that the earliest carriages had to be hauled up and down by using a system of counter-balanced weights: a very hazardous procedure. Though tiny and unspoilt today, Beck Hole was briefly, during the middle of the last century, a busy centre of ironstone mining.

Insight

SALT

Since Anglo-Saxon times salt had been valued for its use in curing meat and fish; it was so valuable that a special tax was levied on it. The River Tees, to the north of the National Park, was the site of important salt pans. Tidal waters were evaporated to leave their salt solution, and salt roads – known as saltersgates – led towards Rievaulx, Old Byland and other monastic communities in the north.

HACKNESS

Steep-sided, wooded valleys fan out from the lovely village of Hackness, which was established at the point where Lowdale Beck meets the River Derwent. It's hard to believe that this secluded spot is only 3 miles (4.8km) from the outskirts of Scarborough. St Hilda, Abbess of Whitby Abbey, established a nunnery here in AD 680, with Abbess Œdilburga; two centuries later Danish invaders razed it to the ground. The

Visit

A SMUGGLERS' TALE

The smuggling of untaxed salt led to a tragedy. An excise man arrived incognito at the Saltersgate Inn, hoping to catch the smugglers 'red-handed'. When his motives were discovered he was quickly murdered and his body hidden behind the fireplace. From that day, almost 200 years ago, the turf fire has never been allowed to go out. It's a nice story; you can still sit by the fire today and decide for yourself whether it's true. Or you can just take it with a pinch of salt...

is the lake, which may have served as a fishery. A more tangible relic, a fragment of an Anglo-Saxon cross, is displayed inside St Peter's Church. Inscriptions, in English, Latin and runic characters, offer up praise to Abbess Œdilburga and prayers for the nuns' own safety. When the cross was carved, possibly in the ninth century, the nuns may have been aware of the fate that awaited them at the hands of marauding Danes.

While Hackness hides in its valley, you can enjoy panoramic views by taking the minor roads to the hilltop villages of Broxa and Silpho. Immediately to the south of Hackness is the Forge Valley, a beautiful, wooded dale created at the end of the Ice Age by glacial meltwater. The River Derwent was diverted from its original direct route, east to the sea at Scalby, to flow south into the Humber.

Forge Valley takes its name from the iron forges, thought to have been worked by the monks of Rievaulx Abbey in the 14th century, fuelled

community rose again in the 11th century, finally to disappear in 1539 on the orders of Henry VIII's Dissolution of the Monasteries.

Hackness Hall (not open to the public), a handsome Georgian house built in 1791 by lord of the manor Sir John Vanden Bempde Johnstone, occupies the site where the nunnery once stood. The only major evidence of that community

by timber felled from this ancient woodland. Today the Forge Valley is a beauty spot and a haven for wildlife. The woods on either side of the river feature native species, including oak, ash, elm and willow, as a pleasant contrast to the regimented conifer plantations that blight rather too many hillsides. Woodpeckers drum insistently; wagtails search for food along the river bank; tiny warblers fill the woods with song each summer. The walking is excellent at any time of year. The popularity of the Forge Valley is emphasised by the provision of car parks and picnic sites. Follow the road southwards through woodlands to emerge at the villages of West and East Ayton, sitting astride the River Derwent and the main A170.

At this point the River Derwent is a mere 4 miles (6.4km) from the seaside resort of Scarborough, yet it still has many miles to flow before it reaches the sea at the mouth of the Humber. The river bridge was constructed in 1775, from stone

Insight

THE GHOST OF HACKNESS

The ghost of Hackness was the invention of an 18th-century vicar's daughter when she found herself a little short of money. She reported seeing a spectral figure that intimated a sum of £50 would allow his soul to be put at rest!

salvaged from the 14th-century castle that once stood near by. Built as a pele tower, a design more commonly found further north, Ayton Castle survives as a ruin.

HOLE OF HORCUM

This remarkable landform, sometimes known locally as the Devil's Punchbowl, is a huge natural amphitheatre seemingly scooped out of Levisham Moor. The valley bottom is primarily pastureland, whilst the steep slopes support superb woods and moorland. Motorists on the A169 Pickering–Whitby road skirt the rim of the Hole of Horcum, and so many

219

stop to gaze in wonderment, and follow some of the good walking paths in the area, that a large car park has been thoughtfully provided.

Many stories account for the origin of the Hole of Horcum; take your pick between the factual and the fanciful. Legend tells that Wade, a local giant, scooped up a handful of earth to throw at his wife, Bell, thus creating the huge landform. Apparently, he missed her and the clod of earth landed to form Blakey Topping, little more than a mile (1.6km) away. To judge from the plethora of folk tales, Wade and his wife spent much of their time tossing missiles at one another. But the origin of the Hole of Horcum is more prosaic, scoured over millennia by glacial meltwater.

Just beyond a steep hairpin bend is the Saltersgate Inn, one of the many solitary inns in the National Park. They were generally sited on junctions of well-used tracks, catering for people on the move, as, indeed, they still do today.

But instead of holiday-makers, those who stood at the bar of the Saltersgate Inn were more likely to have been hauliers leading trains of heavily laden packhorses across the moors, as the inn lies on an old salt road linking the port of Whitby with the market town of Pickering. Later it catered for stagecoach traffic, and was the site of a tollbooth when the road became a turnpike

It is regularly cut off by snow. Photographs displayed in the bar show the pub almost buried beneath drifts. In less inclement weather it's a convenient port of call after walking around the Hole Horcum.

LEVISHAM & LOCKTON

Levisham and Lockton are a pair of very attractive moorland villages lying off the A169, about 5 miles (8km) north of Pickering.

Until 1938 the most prominent feature of Lockton's squat church was an ash tree growing out of the top of the square tower. It was removed and replanted in the

churchyard, but unfortunately it failed to thrive. Apart from that, the village has a youth hostel, a duck pond (sadly, few other village ponds in the National Park have survived intact) and limestone cottages set back from wide grass verges.

Neighbouring Levisham is just amile (1.6km) away, but it is a long mile if you happen to be walking – the villages are divided by a deep gorge. At the bottom, close to Levisham Beck, is a converted watermill and the ruins of St Mary's Church. Though it was built in this isolated spot to be equidistant from both villages, the church can hardly be said to be convenient for either.

Houses, and the Horseshoe Inn, surround a large village green. Pass the pub to join a single track road, with long views along well-wooded Newton Dale. Keep ahead down the road to arrive at Levisham Station, one of the stops for steam trains on the preserved line between Grosmont and Pickering, where the public road ends.

Insight

THE BECK HOLE INCLINE

The section of the original line of the North Yorkshire Railway between Beck Hole and Goathland (bypassed in 1865) consisted of a 1-in-10 incline. Coaches had to be winched up and down with an imaginative arrangement of counter-balanced weights. Primitive though it was, the moorland railway was immediately hailed as a wonder of engineering.

THE NORTH YORKSHIRE MOORS RAILWAY

The North Yorkshire Moors Railway is a remarkable success story. No visit to the moors would be complete without a trip along this most scenic of steam railway lines.

Today the line is purely recreational, but it was commerce and industry that provided the original spur for the line to be built. Two centuries ago Whitby was one of the most important ports

NORTH YORKSHIRE MOORS RAILWAY

75029

DETERMINED ENTHUSIASTS

Wheb Beeching closed the railway line between Pickering and Grosmont in 1965, the story might have ended there, except that a group of enthusiasts, convinced that the line still had a viable future, formed themselves into the North Yorkshire Moors Railway Preservation Society. They raised enough money to buy the trackbed from British Rail and then restored the line and the stations along it. After plenty of hard work, the line was partially reopened in 1969 and from end to end in 1973. Today, it is a popular tourist attraction.

in the country. By the early 1800s, however, the town's traditional industries – whaling, ship building and alum mining – were in decline and Whitby's traders decided that the town needed to improve the communications over land.

In 1831, George Stephenson arrived fresh from his engineering triumphs on the Stockton and Darlington Railway and surveyed the terrain between Whitby and Pickering. His recommendation was for a railway line on which the carriages would be horse-drawn.

An army of navvies was hired in 1833 to drive the line over the moors. Armed only with pick and shovel they tackled the rough terrain. The line from Whitby to Pickering was opened, with the usual fanfare, in 1836, when a trainload of dignitaries was pulled along the track at a sedate 10 miles (16km) per hour.

The line revitalised the area; a variety of industries, such as ironstone mining, sprang up once a regular train service had been established. A few years later it was converted to carry steam engines; the first one chugged into Whitby in 1847. The rather troublesome Beck Hole Incline was bypassed by blasting a new route between Beck Hole and Goathland. By the time a new century dawned the moors and coast were well served with rail links; the trains not only transported goods, they also began to bring visitors from the crowded cities to enjoy the moorland landscape.

In 1965, as a result of the Beeching Reports, nearly 130 years of rail services came to a halt. The Esk Valley line was reprieved, but the section of railway line between Pickering and Grosmont was unceremoniously closed. Eight years of careful restoration and hard work later the line was reopened by the North Yorkshire Moors Railway Preservation Society. More than just another line run by enthusiasts, the North Yorkshire Moors Railway operates a full timetable from March to October.

The 18-mile (29km) rail journey takes visitors into the very heart of the moors. Today, more than 300,000 passenger journeys are taken every year, making the railway the biggest single attraction within the North York Moors National Park. Many travellers board the train at Pickering Station, which dates from 1845 and the advent of steam-hauled trains. Railway enthusiasts will be happy to know that, a century and a half later, the age of steam hasn't disappeared. The line climbs into the spectacular, steep-sided, wooded gorge of Newton Dale, before arriving at Levisham Station. Trains also call at Newtondale Halt, the starting point for a number of waymarked walks.

The next stop is Goathland, which is a favourite destination for visitors, whether travelling by car or rail. With its waterfalls, Rail Trail and delightful moorland setting, the village is well worth exploring. The northern terminus of the North Yorkshire Moors Railway is Grosmont, where travellers can join the main Northern Spirit line between Middlesbrough and Whitby.

PICKERING

The market town of Pickering lies just to the south of the National Park. Overlooking the market place is the large parish church dedicated to Saints Peter and Paul. Hemmed

Visit

MEDIEVAL FRESCOES

The wall paintings in Pickering's church have had a chequered history. They were probably first hidden from view during a bout of puritanical zeal after the Reformation, when such images were considered idolatrous. Rediscovered in 1851, they were almost immediately concealed once again beneath layers of whitewash on the directions of a vicar who shared this puritanical outlook. However, the frescoes were revealed once again in 1878, and are now recognised as some of the best medieval church paintings to be seen in the country.

After the Norman Conquest, King William created outposts in the north to establish order and quell uprisings; Pickering was one of these strategic sites. The first castle was built to a basic motte-and-bailey design; by the 12th century the wooden keep and outer palisade had been rebuilt in stone. It was besieged by Robert the Bruce on one of his incursions south of the border. When the Scots inflicted a heavy defeat on the army led by Edward II in 1322, the King found shelter here.

After this time, the castle saw no further military action, and was used by a succession of monarchs as a hunting lodge. Some parts of the forest are still royal property, but Pickering Castle is maintained by English Heritage.

Beck Isle Museum close to Pickering Beck, offers glimpses into the more recent past. Successive rooms are devoted to bygone life in town and country; you can visit the cobblers, gents' outfitters, kitchen, barber's shop and a public house.

in by houses and shops, the building is approached by gates (streets) and ginnels (alleys). Inside are 15th-century frescoes, illustrating scenes from the lives of saints and martyrs. St George slays a dragon; Thomas Becket expires in the cathedral; St Edmund raises his eyes towards heaven as arrows pierce his flesh.

Outbuildings house a blacksmith's forge and wheelwright.

RAVENSCAR

Great things were planned for Ravenscar. A developer called John Septimus Bland decided to build a holiday resort that he thought would rival Whitby and Scarborough. A station was built, Bland laid out the town's network of roads and began to build shops and houses. But Bland's company went bankrupt, and work stopped. Despite the panoramic sea views, this exposed site was clearly unsuitable for such a development. It is geologically unstable, and visitors would have been faced with an awkward descent to the stony beach far below.

You can see Ravenscar's street layout today, though grass grows where buildings ought to have been. When the Raven Hall Hotel was built in 1774, it was simply Raven Hall. The hotel was to have been the centrepiece of the resort; now it stands alone, its mock battlements a landmark for miles around.

The Romans built a signal station here; its foundations and an inscribed stone (on display in Whitby's Pannett Park Museum) were found when Raven Hall's own foundations were laid. The signal station relayed warnings of Anglo-Saxon invaders to military bases.

Visit & Activity

RAVENSCAR'S COASTLINE

The fault-line that runs along the coast between Boulby and Scarborough is most clearly visible at Ravenscar. At low tide the rocky shoreline is revealed as a series of concentric curves, formed from layers of hard and soft rock, eroded by the waves over millions of years. This is excellent walking country, on either the beach or cliff-top. The Cleveland Way and the trackbed of the old Whitby–Scarborough railway, open to walkers and cyclists, are near by. Ravenscar is also the finish to the 42-mile (67.2km) hike across the moors from Osmotherley known as the Lyke Wake Walk.

This part of the coastline (National Trust, Coastal Centre in Ravenscar) was exploited in the 17th century for alum, used in dyeing to fix colours permanently. Remains of the quarries and buildings can be found near Ravenscar.

ROBIN HOOD'S BAY

Robin Hood's Bay vies with Staithes for the title of prettiest fishing village on Yorkshire's coastline. Both communities have to juggle the conflicting demands of tourism with the needs of local people. To visit Robin Hood's Bay be sure to leave your car at the top of the hill, where there are two large car parks. The road down to the beach is a cul-de-sac and visitors' cars are barred.

Apart from the access road, the houses – which cling precariously to the side of the cliff – are reached by narrow alleyways and steps. The result is a jumble of whitewashed cottages and red-tiled roofs leading down the main street and almost into the sea. An old story tells of a ship which at high tide came so close to shore that its bowsprit knocked out the window of a pub!

There is no harbour. Where once there were more than a hundred fishing boats, there are now just a handful, and they are launched down a slipway. Many of the old fishermen's cottages are now holiday homes. There is a good stretch of sandy beach and a rocky foreshore; children love to investigate the little rock pools left in these scars by the receding tide. Take care; it is easy to get cut off by the tide when it starts coming in again.

Robin Hood's Bay has had its share of storms, their effects exacerbated by the softness of the rock that forms the cliffs. A sea wall helps to blunt the worst of the buffeting, though every winter still brings memorable storms.

The only community of any size between Whitby and Scarborough, the relative isolation of Robin Hood's Bay helped to make it a haunt of smugglers. It used to be said that

a boat-load of contraband could be beached, and the load transferred to the top of the village through a maze of secret passages between the tightly packed houses, all without seeing the light of day.

You can walk at low tide along the beach (keep an eye out for the incoming tide) to Ravenscar, high on its cliff-top to the south, or along a lovely section of the Cleveland Way. On your way, about a mile (1.6km) from Robin Hood's Bay, is Boggle Hole, a little wooded cove. An old water mill, which was once powered by Mill Beck and is now a youth hostel conveniently situated for walkers on Cleveland Wayfarers.

SCARBOROUGH

The well-loved resort of Scarborough can claim to be one of the oldest in the country. Its prosperity can be traced back to the occasion in the year 1620, when a visitor, Mrs Elizabeth Farrow, was drinking a glass of spring water. Finding the water acidic in taste, she came to the natural conclusion that something that tasted so unpleasant must surely have medicinal qualities.

Promises of miraculous cures have always had willing ears, the more outlandish the better. Scarborough's spring water was said to cure many ills, even hypochondria: surely a rather self-defeating exercise, since hypochondriacs were precisely the sort of people to whom the town extended the warmest welcome. Scarborough's spring water certainly contains Epsom salts and a cocktail of minerals. It was definitely good for one thing – giving the town's economy a much-needed shot in the arm. The taking of the waters was soon put on a more commercial footing. Scarborough became known as a spa town; a name borrowed from the Belgian resort. Scarborough was put firmly on the map as a place where the well-heeled might come to recuperate at leisure. Emboldened by this success, a local doctor started to extol the health-giving properties of sea bathing. One way or another Scarborough's waters were responsible for its success.

The first spa house was built over the original spa well in 1700. However, it was to suffer the fate shared by many other Scarborough buildings, by falling into the sea. Ever more elaborate spa houses were built, each one getting the royal stamp of approval for the water's efficacy. By the time Queen Victoria ascended to the throne, Scarborough was arguably the north's finest resort; many of the town's most distinguished buildings date from Victoria's reign. The Grand Hotel, overlooking the South Bay sums up the prosperity of Scarborough during the busiest time in its long history.

Scarborough Castle has dominated the town with an air of fortress-like impregnability for the best part of a millennium. Standing proudly on its headland, between the North and South Bays, it enjoys an uninterrupted view over the town and out to sea. Remains of even earlier

Insight

A MIRACULOUS CURE

Elaborate claims were made for the many ailments which Scarborough's spring waters might cure. Once stomach ache, consumption, rheumatism and fever had been taken care of, the waters would sort out palsy, madness and leprosy.

defences have been unearthed, including an Iron-Age settlement and a Roman signal station.

The Norman edifice dates back to 1136, when William de Gros decided to rebuild in stone an earlier wooden fort. Henry II, concerned that many of his noblemen were growing too powerful, set about destroying their castles. He spared Scarborough, however. Impressed by its air of impregnability, he requisitioned the castle and kept it.

Besieged on a number of occasions, Scarborough Castle was never taken by force, but attacking forces managed to starve the

Insight

AN IMPREGNABLE FORTRESS

Scarborough Castle has never been taken by force. When the castle was besieged by the Roundheads in 1645 a deep well provided a good supply of fresh water for the Royalist inhabitants. However, the beleaguered soldiers inside the castle eventually ran out of food, and were reduced to eating rats and deriving what little sustenance was available by boiling up their leather belts and boots.

defenders into surrendering. On one occasion, in 1645, Hugh Chomley's Royalist troops were besieged by John Meldrum's Scottish army and the Great Keep was damaged by the Scottish artillery. Unable to hold out any longer, they were allowed to surrender with honour intact; those men who could still stand were allowed to march out of the castle. The castle was beseiged again in 1648 when the Parliamentary garrison, discontented because they

had not been paid, went over to the King's side; they too were starved into submission.

St Mary's Church also suffered artillery damage at the hands of the Royalists defending the castle, which is still visible. Anne Brontë was visiting Scarborough in 1849 when she succumbed to tuberculosis and died. She is buried in the churchyard.

While many British resorts have lost out to the ease of foreign travel, Scarborough has enough attractions to keep the most fastidious visitors coming back. Cricket lovers eagerly anticipate the Scarborough Festival, held towards the end of the season. Playwright Sir Alan Ayckbourn keeps faith with local theatre-goers by premièring most of his plays here in his Stephen Joseph Theatre before they transfer to London's West End. The miniature North Bay Railway runs for just under a mile (1.6km) between Peasholme Park and the Sealife Centre at Scalby Mills, where there is a Caribbean-style coral reef, fish galore, turtles and sharks.

SCARBOROUGH CASTLE

EASTERN MOORS & COAST

SLEIGHTS

Sleights straddles the River Esk in a sheltered dip in the landscape, just outside the boundary of the National Park. There are few buildings here to attract the eye, but it is a convenient spot from which to explore the surrounding countryside – whether you head for open moorland, or the more intimate environs of the Esk.

Ruswarp, inside the National Park, between Sleights and the sea, marks the tidal limit of the River Esk. Here, on a quiet stretch of the river, you can hire a dinghy.

A minor road from Sleights leads to a hamlet that glories in the name of Ugglebarnby. The meaning is 'the farm of old owl beard'; the explanation is less easy to fathom. Continue past Ugglebarnby to arrive in Littlebeck, on a road that snakes through this delightful village. Here you can enjoy fine walks, one along May Beck and the other to the south to see Falling Foss, an exquisite waterfall in a woodland setting.

THORNTON-LE-DALE

Despite being split in two by the busy A170, Thornton-le-Dale is still said to be one of the prettiest villages in Yorkshire. The thatched cottage beside Dalby Beck makes regular appearances on calendars and biscuit-tin lids. The boundary of the National Park makes a little detour to include the village – a good indication that it is worth making a stop here. Try to time your visit outside the busier holiday periods.

FALLING FOSS

The tone is established by the beck; its meandering course through the village is punctuated by a succession of tiny bridges. At the crossroads, in the centre of the village, is a small green where the slender, stepped market cross and a set of wooden stocks still stand. On the opposite side of the road are Lady Lumley's Almshouses, a block of twelve dwellings, built in 1670 and still retaining their original use. The churchyard is the burial place of Matthew Grimes, who died in 1875 at the grand old age of 96. His claim to fame is that he guarded Napoleon during the emperor's exile on the island of St Helena, and helped to carry his body to the grave. Thornton-le-Dale's churchyard is also the last resting place of Sir Richard Chomley, known as The Great Black Knight of the North. He served at the court of Elizabeth I; his home, Roxby Castle, once stood just to the west of Thornton-le-Dale. His effigy can be seen inside the church. In Ellerburn, just to the north, is the

Insight

SUPERSTITIONS

Superstitions were rife in rural areas. Charms considered to be lucky included a horseshoe (or stone with a natural hole in it), hung from the door of the house. Picking up a pin, or other piece of metal, would prevent a witch from using it in her spells. The rowan tree was also known as witchwood; carrying a crucifix made of rowan wood was a common way to guard against the 'evil eye'.

tiny Church of St Hilda, where you'll find many examples of Viking stone work, including several cross heads and a serpent sculpture.

To explore further afield take the Forest Drive (toll payable) through Dalby Forest, which is easily accessible by driving north from Thornton-le-Dale, where there are numerous pleasant walking trails, mountain-bike routes, fishing areas and picnic places, a useful visitor centre and shop.

TOURIST INFORMATION CENTRES

Pickering
The Ropery.
Tel: 01751 473791

Scarborough
Brunswick Shopping Centre,
Westborough.
Tel: 01723 383636
Harbourside, Sandside.
Tel: 01723 383636 (seasonal)

PLACES OF INTEREST

Beck Isle Museum
Bridge Street, Pickering.
Tel: 01751 473653;
www.beckislemuseum.co.uk

Crescent Arts Workshop
The Crescent, Scarborough.
Tel: 01723 351461;
www.crescentarts.co.uk

National Trust Centre
Ravenscar.
Tel: 01723 870138 or 870423

North Yorkshire Moors Railway
Pickering Station, Pickering.
Tel: 01751 472508;
www.northyorkshiremoorsrailway.com

The Old Coastguard Station Visitor Centre
Robin Hood's Bay.
Tel: 01947 885900

Pickering Castle
Tel: 01751 474989

Robin Hood's Bay Museum
Fisherhead.

The Rotunda Museum
Vernon Road, Scarborough.
www.rotundamuseum.org.uk

Scarborough Art Gallery
The Crescent.
Tel: 01723 374753;
www.scarboroughmuseums.org.uk

Scarborough Castle
Tel: 01723 372451

Sea Life & Marine Sanctuary
Scalby Mills, Scarborough.
Tel: 01723 376125;
www.sealifeeurope.com

Staintondale Shire Horse Farm
Staintondale.
Tel: 01723 870458;
www.shirehorsefarm.co.uk

Woodend Natural History Museum
The Crescent, Scarborough.
Tel: 01723 367326;
www. scarboroughmuseums.org.uk

FOR CHILDREN
Staintondale Shire Horse Farm
Staintondale.
Tel: 01723 870458;
www.shirehorsefarm.co.uk

SHOPPING
MARKET
Open-air market, Pickering, Mon.

LOCAL SPECIALITIES
Ceramics
Green Man Gallery, 8 Park Street,
Pickering. Tel: 01751 472361
Honey
The Honey Farm, East Ayton.
Tel: 01723 865198
Ice-Cream
Beacon Farm, Beacon Way, Sneaton.
Tel: 01947 605212;
www.beacon-farm.co.uk

Trout
Moorland Trout Farm, Pickering.
Tel: 01751 473101

PERFORMING ARTS
Futurist Theatre and Cinema
Foreshore Road, Scarborough.
Tel: 01723 365789;
www.futuristtheatre.co.uk
Spa Entertainment Complex
South Bay, Scarborough.
Tel: 01723 376774;
www.scarboroughspa.co.uk
Spa Theatre
South Bay, Scarborough.
Tel: 01723 357869
Stephen Joseph Theatre
Westborough, Scarborough.
Tel: 01723 370541;
www.sjt.uk.com

SPORTS & ACTIVITIES
ANGLING
Sea
Boats for hire at the harbour in South Bay, Scarborough.
Fly
Pickering Trout Lake.
Tel: 01751 474219
The Mere, Scarborough.
Day tickets on site.
Wykeham Trout Lakes (coarse and trout).
Tel: 07946 534001;
www.dawnay.co.uk
BEACHES
There are sandy beaches with easy access at Robin Hood's Bay and Scarborough.
CRICKET
Scarborough
North Marine Road.
Tel: 01723 365625
GOLF COURSES
Kirkbymoorside
Kirkbymoorside Golf Club, Manor Vale.
Tel: 01751 431525

Scarborough
North Cliff Golf Club, North Cliff Avenue.
Tel: 01723 360786.
South Cliff Golf Club, Deepdale Avenue.
Tel: 01723 365150
CYCLE HIRE
Dalby
Purple Mountain Bike Hire, The Courtyard, Low Dalby.
Tel 01751 460011;
www.purplemountain.co.uk
HORSE-RIDING
Robin Hood's Bay
Farsyde Stud and Riding Centre.
Tel: 01947 880249;
www.farsydefarmcottages.co.uk
Snainton
Snainton Riding Centre.
Tel: 01723 859218;
www.snaintonridingcentre.co.uk
Staintondale Pony Trekking Centre.
Tel: 01723 871846
LLAMA TREKKING
Staintondale
Wellington Lodge Llamas.
Tel: 01723 871234;
www.llamatreks.co.uk

LONO-DISTANCE TRAILS & FOOTPATHS

Moor to Sea

80-mile (129km) cycle route linking Pickering, Scarborough and Whitby; www.moortoseacycle.net

The Rail Trail

A 3.5-mile (5.6km) walk from Goathland to Grosmont following the track bed of George Stephenson's original railway line.

Scarborough to Whitby Railway Trail

Route for walkers and cyclists follows the old railway line. (Cycle hire at Hawsker.)

FORESTS

Dalby Forest Drive. Free for pedestrians, cyclists and Moorsbus passengers.
Dalby Forest Visitor Centre and shop.
Tel: 01751 472771

ANNUAL EVENTS & CUSTOMS

Littlebeck

Littlebeck Rose Queen Ceremony, Aug.

Pickering

Jazz Festival, Jul.
Traction Engine Rally, Aug.

Robin Hood's Bay

Folk Festival, Jun.

Scalby

Scalby Fair, early Jun.

Scarborough

Scarborough Fayre, Jun.
International Music Festival, Jun.
Scarborough Cricket Festival, end Aug/Sep.

Thornton-le-Dale

Thornton-le-Dale Show, Aug.

TEA ROOMS

Foxcliffe Tea Rooms

Station Square, Ravenscar,
YO13 0LU
Tel: 01723 871028

With twelve varieties of tea and six blends of coffee, the Foxcliffe offers a wide choice. Based in one of the few buildings – part of the station – that were erected in what was planned to be a coastal resort to rival Scarborough, the café offers delicious home-baked cakes and hot food – and spectacular cliff-top and sea views.

The Mallyan Spout Hotel

The Common, Goathland,
YO22 5AN
Tel. 01947 896486
www.mallyanspout.co.uk

You could bump into the stars of television's Heartbeat while you have afternoon tea at the Mallyan Spout. Choose from scones, delicious cakes and sandwiches, or a more substantial meal from the selection that's served all day. Relax in the lounge or enjoy the garden and patio.

The Old Bakery Tea Rooms

Chapel Street, Robin Hood's Bay,
YO22 4SQ
Tel: 01947 880709

A lovely, traditional tea room, situated in the heart of the village. The bread and cakes are produced in the attached bakery. Scones with home-made preserves are a favourite, along with the chocolate and coffee cakes. There's an enclosed balcony overlooking the stream – a good place to rest and watch the world go by.

Warrington House

Whitbygate, Thornton-le-Dale,
YO18 7RY
Tel: 01751 475028
www.warringtonhouse.co.uk

Just a few yards from the bustling centre of Thornton-le-Dale, this tea room is the place to enjoy afternoon tea with a selection of home-made cakes and scones, a ploughman's lunch or vegetable strudel. There's a delicious array of puddings on offer, too,

RAVENSCAR

Birch Hall Inn
Beckhole, Goathland, YO22 5LE
Tel: 01947 896245

The Birch Hall is a bit off the beaten track, though near the North Yorkshire Moors Railway line. But it's worth persevering to find it, as it's real gem. There's nothing flashy about it, but if you like real local ales properly kept and served, wholesome food like tasty pies, substantial sandwiches and their own delicious beer cake, this is the place to come.

Laurel Inn
New Road, Robin Hood's Bay, YO22 4SE
Tel: 01947 880400

Near to the bottom of the winding main street, this pub has a cosy, traditional atmosphere, with an open fire. It offers real ales and simple but wholesome food – including tasty thick soups in the winter.

Moorcock Inn
Langdale End, Scarborough, YO13 0BN
Tel: 01723 882268

This remote Moors pub has a tiled floor and a rather odd assortment of benches in two small rooms. However, you're guaranteed a decent drink, with a changing selection of beer from local regional and micro-breweries. In the summer, home-cooked food is available, and you can sit outside in good weather.

The New Inn
Moorgate, Thornton-le-Dale, YO28 7LF
Tel: 01751 474226
www.the-new-inn.com

This fine Georgian building at the heart of the village retains its traditional atmosphere, with log fires and hand-pulled beer. There is a flower-filled patio on which to enjoy a drink, while the restaurant offers a wide range of meals using fresh, local ingredients.

USEFUL INFORMATION

NORTH YORK MOORS NATIONAL PARK INFORMATION POINTS

North York Moors National Park
The Old Vicarage, Bondgate, Helmsley.
Tel: 01439 770657;
www.northyorkmoors-npa.gov.uk
Useful Websites
www.north-york-moors.com;
www.yorkshirenet.co.uk;
www.york-moors.co.uk

OTHER INFORMATION

Angling

Numerous opportunities for fishing on farms, lakes and rivers. Permits and licences are available from local tackle shops and TICs.

Coastguard

Dial 999 and ask for the Coastguard Service, which co-ordinates rescue services.

English Heritage

Canada House, 3 Chepstow Street, Manchester.
Tel: 0161 242 1400;
www.english-heritage.org.uk

English Heritage (Yorkshire)

37 Tanner Row, York.
Tel: 01904 601901

Environment Agency

Rivers House, 21 Park Sq South, Leeds.
Tel: 0113 2440191

Forest Enterprise

Outgang Road, Pickering.
Tel: 01751 472771

Health

Information on health problems is available from NHS Direct.
Tel: 0845 4647; www.nhsdirect.nhs.uk

Dental Helpline

Tel: 0845 063 1188
Moorsbus Summer Coach and Minibus
Tel 01439 77065; www.moorsbus.net

The National Trust

Goddards, 27 Tadcaster Road, York.

Tel: 01904 702021;

www.nationaltrust.org.uk

Parking

Information on parking permits and car parks in the area is available from local TICs.

Places of Interest

We give details of just some of the facilities within the area covered by this guide. Further information can be obtained from local TICs or the web.

Yorkshire Tourist Board

312 Tadcaster Road, York.

Tel: 01904 707961;

www.ytb.org.uk

Yorkshire Wildlife Trust

10 Toft Green, York.

Tel: 01904 659570;

www.yorkshire-wildlife-trust.org.uk

INDEX

INDEX

ACKNOWLEDGEMENTS

The Automobile Association would like to thank the following photographers, companies and picture libraries for their assistance in the preparation of this book.

Abbreviations for the picture credits are as follows. (t) top; (b) bottom; (l) left; (r) right; (AA) AA World Travel Library.

2/3 AA/R Czaja; 5 AA/ M Kipling; 6 AA/M Kipling; 9 AA/M Kipling; 12 AA/M Kipling; 13 AA/M Kipling; 14 AA/M Kipling; 15l, 15r AA/M Kipling; 16 AA/M Kipling; 17 AA/M Kipling; 19 AA/M Kipling; 20 AA/J Morrison; 23 AA/M Kipling; 24 AA/M Kipling; 26 AA/M Kipling; 28/9 AA/M Kipling; 30 AA/M Kipling; 31t, 31b AA/M Kipling; 33 AA/M Kipling; 34 AA/M Kipling; 37 AA/M Kipling; 38 AA/M Kipling; 41 AA/J Morrison; 42/3 AA/M Kipling; 44 AA/J Morrison; 47 AA/M Kipling; 48 AA/M Kipling; 50/1 AA/M Kipling; 53 AA/M Kipling; 54 AA/M Kipling; 57 AA/M Kipling; 58/9 AA/M Kipling; 60 AA/M Kipling; 63 AA/M Kipling; 64 AA/M Kipling; 66/7 AA/M Kipling; 69 AA/M Kipling; 70/1 AA/M Kipling; 74 AA/M Kipling; 78/9 AA/L Whitwam; 87 AA/M Kipling; 88 AA/M Kipling; 90 AA/M Kipling; 92/3 AA/J Morrison; 94 AA/M Kipling; 95t AA/S Gregory; 95b AA/C Mellor; 96 AA/M Kipling; 98/9 AA/J Morrison; 100 AA/M Kipling; 102/3 AA/M Kipling; 106/7 AA/J Morrison; 110 AA/M Kipling; 113 AA/M Kipling; 114/5 AA/M Kipling; 117 AA/R Newton; 118/9 AA/M Kipling; 122/3 AA/M Kipling; 124 AA/M Kipling; 126/7 AA/M Kipling; 129 AA/M Kipling; 131 S & O Mathews; 132 AA/J Morrison; 134/5 AA/M Kipling; 139 AA/M Kipling; 143 AA/M Kipling; 146/7 AA/M Kipling; 151 AA/M Kipling; 152 AA/M Kipling; 154 AA/J Morrison; 156/7 AA/J Morrison; 158 AA/M Kipling; 159 AA/L Whitwam; 160t, 160b AA/L Whitwam; 161 AA/M Kipling; 163 AA/M Kipling; 165 AA/M Kipling; 166/7 AA/M Kipling; 170 AA/J Morrison; 173 AA/M Kipling; 174/5 AA/M Kipling; 178 AA/R Newton; 181 AA/M Kipling; 182/3 AA/M Kipling; 185 AA/M Kipling; 187 AA/M Kipling; 188 AA/M Kipling; 195 AA/M Kipling; 196 AA/M Kipling; 198 AA/M Kipling; 200/1 AA/L Whitwam; 202 AA/M Kipling; 203 AA/M Kipling; 204l, 204r AA/M Kipling; 205 AA/J Morrison; 207 AA/J Morrison; 208 AA/T Mackie; 210/1 AA/M Kipling; 213 AA/M Kipling; 214 AA/M Kipling; 217 AA/M Kipling; 218 AA/M Kipling; 221 AA/J Morrison; 223 AA/M Kipling; 227 AA/M Kipling; 230/1 AA/M Kipling; 234/5 AA/P Wilson; 237 AA/T Woodcock; 239 AA/M Kipling; 240 AA/L Whitwam; 247 AA/M Kipling; 249 AA/J Morrison.

Every effort has been made to trace the copyright holders, and we apologise in advance for any accidental errors. We would be happy to apply the corrections in the following edition of this publication.